AMIGURUMI TOY BOX

cute crocheted friends

Ana Paula Rímoli

Martingale®
& COMPANY

Amigurumi Toy Box:
Cute Crocheted Friends
© 2011 by Ana Paula Rímoli

Martingale
& COMPANY

Martingale & Company
19021 120th Ave. NE, Ste. 102
Bothell, WA 98011-9511 USA
www.martingale-pub.com

Printed in China
16 15 14 13 12 11   8 7 6 5 4 3 2 1

**Library of Congress
Cataloging-in-Publication Data
is available upon request.**

ISBN: 978-1-60468-045-4

MISSION STATEMENT
Dedicated to providing quality products and service to inspire creativity.

CREDITS

President & CEO: Tom Wierzbicki

Editor in Chief: Mary V. Green

Managing Editor: Tina Cook

Developmental Editor:
    Karen Costello Soltys

Technical Editor: Ursula Reikes

Copy Editor: Sheila Chapman Ryan

Design Director: Stan Green

Production Manager: Regina Girard

Illustrator: Laurel Strand

Cover & Text Designer: Regina Girard

Photographer: Brent Kane

DEDICATION

Para las nenas más lindas del mundo: Oli y Marti—las quiero mucho mucho—y para Franco, que me banca y me quiere y me cuida—te amo.

ACKNOWLEDGMENTS

I'd like to thank Karen Soltys for putting up with all my random ideas and for being so trusting. Thank you for letting me keep dreaming!

Thank you, Ursula Reikes, for making the patterns so clear, for being right all the time (I think she can read my mind!), and for making sure the books are perfect.

And thank you to everybody else at Martingale & Company; you're the nicest people to work with and I am more than grateful for everything you do to make my toys look so good (Brent Kane takes the cutest pictures!) and the books so pretty. I know it takes a lot of people to make such beautiful work. Thank you very much to all of you. I really appreciate it.

CONTENTS

iNTRODUCTiON

My daughters are growing up so fast! As I was writing this book, Oli turned seven, and Marti turned four. They have a very interesting love-hate relationship (a lot more love than hate!). Oli likes to have her things all neat and organized and Martina believes that absolutely everything on the planet belongs to her, so there's no convincing her that she shouldn't draw in Olivia's journal, for example, or cut her sister's magazines into tiny little pieces that you find everywhere for days (including in our bed, Santiago's water bowl, and even the pantry!). These incidents are always followed by a lot of yelling (Martina) and heartfelt sobbing (Oli).

But then, after some talking, Marti says she's sorry and Oli says it's all right, and they hug and play games and smile and make me want to kiss them forever. I hope they'll be best friends when they grow up, and that the arguing (always followed by making up) will only make their bond grow stronger.

I had fun imagining the friendships and activities of the little toys when working on this book. I figured that dolphins, narwhals, and jellyfish have to be the best of friends, swimming together in the ocean, and that our new garden is full of little creatures playing hide-and-seek all afternoon. There's a cute hot-dog set and little snacks that

are super fun to play with; some moms and babies, including a polar-bear pair that likes to go fishing together; and even a happy tree full of tiny leaves.

I really hope you'll have fun crocheting the projects in this book, and that they'll inspire new crocheters to pick up a hook and start making the world a little cuter, one little toy at a time!

Thank you very much, as always, for being so nice and liking my work. Happy, happy crocheting!

~Ana

HOT-DOG SET

In Uruguay we call hot dogs *panchos*.
They were my favorite food when I was growing up, but
I would eat them with mashed potatoes instead of a bun! The
girls love to play with their *pancho* set, and they have lots of fun
pretending to sell and buy them and asking each other if they want
ketchup or mayonnaise (they don't like mustard).

FINISHED SIZES

Bun: Approx 6" long

Hot dog: Approx 7" long

Mustard bottle: Approx 3" tall

Ketchup bottle: Approx 4¾" tall

MATERIALS

Worsted-weight yarn in white, tan, burgundy, red, and yellow

Size G/6 (4 mm) crochet hook

6 and 9 mm plastic eyes with safety backings

Small pieces of yellow and red craft felt

Sewing thread and sharp needle

Black embroidery floss and embroidery needle

Tapestry needle

Fiberfill or stuffing of your choice

BUN

The bread is crocheted in the round—well, more like "in the oval."

Bottom (Make 2.)

These will look like two little canoes.

Using tan yarn, loosely ch 21.

R1: Sc 20 starting at second bump at back of ch (see page 76), and then sc 20 on opposite side of ch (both loops of ch). (40 sts)

R2: *Sc 4 in next sc, sc 19*, rep once. (46 sts)

R3: *Sc 2 in each of next 3 sc, sc 20*, rep once. (52 sts)

R4: *Sc 2 in each of next 4 sc, sc 22*, rep once. (60 sts)

R5: *Sc 2 in each of next 5 sc, sc 25*, rep once. (72 sts)

R6–10: Sc 70.

Fasten off and set aside.

Top (Make 2.)

These will look like surfboards.

Using white yarn, rep instructions for bottom through R5.

R6: Sc 70.

Fasten off, leaving long tail for sewing.

With WS tog, align sts of 1 bottom with sts of 1 top and sew tog, stuffing as you go (don't worry if the top looks smaller than the bottom, because they're the same amount of sts; once you start sewing, it'll look perfect). When both sides of the bun are done, use tan yarn to sew 2 halves tog along sides (so they look like a real hot-dog bun).

HOT DOG (EL PANCHO!)

Using burgundy yarn,

R1: Ch 2, 5 sc in second ch from hook.

R2: Sc 2 in each sc around. (10 sts)

R3: *Sc 1, sc 2 in next sc*, rep 5 times. (15 sts)

R4–12: Sc 15.

Work on face: Position and attach 6 mm eyes; embroider mouth. For cheeks, use the pattern to cut 2 circles from yellow felt and sew to face.

R13–40: Sc 15, stuffing as you go.

R41: *Sc 1, dec 1*, rep 5 times. (10 sts)

R42: Dec 5 times. (5 sts)

Fasten off, leaving long tail to close up 5-st hole.

MUSTARD BOTTLE

Using yellow yarn,

R1: Ch 2, 6 sc in second ch from hook.

R2: Sc 2 in each st around. (12 sts)

R3: *Sc 1, 2 sc in next st*, rep 6 times. (18 sts)

R4: *Sc 2, 2 sc in next st*, rep 6 times. (24 sts)

R5: *Sc 3, 2 sc in next st*, rep 6 times. (30 sts)

R6: *Sc 4, 2 sc in next st*, rep 6 times. (36 sts)

R7: Through back loops only, *sc 4, dec 1*, rep 6 times. (30 sts)

R8–16: Sc 30.

R17: Sc 30 through back loops only.

R18: *Sc 3, dec 1*, rep 6 times. (24 sts)

R19: *Sc 2, dec 1*, rep 6 times. (18 sts)

Work on face: Position and attach 9 mm eyes; embroider mouth. For cheeks, use the pattern to cut 2 circles from red felt and sew to face.

R20: *Sc 1, dec 1*, rep 6 times. (12 sts)

R21: Sc 12.

Stuff almost to top.

R22: Dec 6 times. (6 sts)

R23: Sc 6.

Sl st 1 and fasten off, leaving long tail to close up 6-st hole.

KETCHUP BOTTLE

Using red yarn,

R1: Ch 2, 6 sc in second ch from hook.

R2: Sc 2 in each st around. (12 sts)

R3: *Sc 1, 2 sc in next st*, rep 6 times. (18 sts)

R4: *Sc 2, 2 sc in next st*, rep 6 times. (24 sts)

R5: *Sc 3, 2 sc in next st*, rep 6 times. (30 sts)

R6: Through back loops only, *sc 3, dec 1*, rep 6 times. (24 sts)

R7–24: Sc 24.

Work on face: Position and attach 9 mm eyes; embroider mouth.

R25: Sc 24 through back loops only.

R26: *Sc 2, dec 1*, rep 6 times. (18 sts)

R27: *Sc 1, dec 1*, rep 6 times. (12 sts)

R28: Sc 12.

Stuff almost to top.

R29: Dec 6 times. (6 sts)

R30: Sc 6.

Sl st 1 and fasten off, leaving long tail to close up 6-st hole.

Hot dog cheek

Mustard bottle cheek

MOM and BaBY POLaR BeaR

I enjoy spending time doing things together with
my girls. Oli loves sewing buttons on little pieces of fabric,
embroidering, and crocheting. (You should see my glowing face right
now.) Martina loves to help me bake, and also likes drawing and
playing with dolls. I bet you that mom and baby polar
bears just love to fish together!

FINISHeD SiZes

Mom polar bear: Approx 5½" tall
Baby polar bear: Approx 3½" tall

MaTeRiaLs

Worsted-weight yarn in white, orange,
green, gray, and brown

Size G/6 (4 mm) and F/5 (3.75 mm)
crochet hooks (use G hook unless
otherwise instructed)

9 and 12 mm plastic eyes with safety
backings

Small piece of blue craft felt

Black embroidery floss and embroidery
needle

Tapestry needle

Fiberfill or stuffing of your choice

1 pipe cleaner

MOM POLaR BeaR

Use white yarn throughout for Mom.

Muzzle

R1: Ch 2, 5 sc in second ch from hook.

R2: Sc 2 in each sc around. (10 sts)

R3: *Sc 1, 2 sc in next sc*, rep 5 times.
(15 sts)

R4: Sc 15.

Sl st 1 and fasten off, leaving long tail for
sewing. Embroider nose and mouth
and set aside.

Head

R1: Ch 2, 5 sc in second ch from hook.

R2: Sc 2 in each sc around. (10 sts)

R3: *Sc 1, 2 sc in next sc*, rep 5 times.
(15 sts)

R4: *Sc 2, 2 sc in next sc*, rep 5 times.
(20 sts)

R5: *Sc 3, 2 sc in next sc*, rep 5 times.
(25 sts)

R6: *Sc 4, 2 sc in next sc*, rep 5 times. (30 sts)

R7: *Sc 5, 2 sc in next sc*, rep 5 times. (35 sts)

R8: *Sc 6, 2 sc in next sc*, rep 5 times. (40 sts)

R9–17: Sc 40.

R18: *Sc 6, dec 1*, rep 5 times. (35 sts)

R19: *Sc 5, dec 1*, rep 5 times. (30 sts)

R20: *Sc 4, dec 1*, rep 5 times. (25 sts)

Work on face: Use the pattern on page 15 to cut 2 circles from blue felt. Cut small slit in middle of each circle, insert 12 mm eyes, and secure to head. Stuff muzzle a little and sew to face.

R21: *Sc 3, dec 1*, rep 5 times. (20 sts)

R22: *Sc 2, dec 1*, rep 5 times. (15 sts)

Stuff head.

R23: *Sc 1, dec 1*, rep 5 times. (10 sts)

R24: Dec 5 times. (5 sts)

Fasten off, and set aside.

Ears (Make 2.)

R1: Ch 2, 6 sc in second ch from hook.

R2 and 3: Sc 6.

Sl st 1 and fasten off, leaving long tail for sewing. Sew open end tog and sew to head.

Body

R1: Ch 2, 5 sc in second ch from hook.

R2: Sc 2 in each sc around. (10 sts)

R3: *Sc 1, 2 sc in next sc*, rep 5 times. (15 sts)

R4: *Sc 2, 2 sc in next sc*, rep 5 times. (20 sts)

R5: *Sc 3, 2 sc in next sc*, rep 5 times. (25 sts)

R6–17: Sc 25.

Sl st 1 and fasten off, leaving long tail for sewing. Stuff and sew to head.

Arms and Legs (Make 4.)

R1: Ch 2, 5 sc in second ch from hook.

R2: Sc 2 in each sc around. (10 sts)

R3–10: Sc 10.

Fasten off, leaving long tail for sewing. Stuff, sew open end tog, and sew to body.

BABY POLAR BEAR

Use white yarn throughout for Baby.

Muzzle

R1: Ch 2, 6 sc in second ch from hook.

R2: Sc 2 in each sc around. (12 sts)

R3: Sc 12.

Sl st 1 and fasten off, leaving long tail for sewing. Embroider nose and mouth and set aside.

Head

R1: Ch 2, 5 sc in second ch from hook.

R2: Sc 2 in each sc around. (10 sts)

R3: *Sc 1, 2 sc in next sc*, rep 5 times. (15 sts)

R4: *Sc 2, 2 sc in next sc*, rep 5 times. (20 sts)

R5: *Sc 3, 2 sc in next sc*, rep 5 times. (25 sts)

R6: *Sc 4, 2 sc in next sc*, rep 5 times. (30 sts)

R7–13: Sc 30.

R14: *Sc 4, dec 1*, rep 5 times. (25 sts)

Work on face: Position and attach 9 mm eyes; stuff muzzle a little and sew to face.

R15: *Sc 3, dec 1*, rep 5 times. (20 sts)

R16: *Sc 2, dec 1*, rep 5 times. (15 sts)

Stuff head.

R17: *Sc 1, dec 1*, rep 5 times. (10 sts)

R18: Dec 5 times. (5 sts)

Fasten off, and set aside.

Ears (Make 2.)

R1: Ch 2, 5 sc in second ch from hook.

R2 and 3: Sc 5.

Sl st 1 and fasten off, leaving long tail for sewing. Sew open end tog and sew to head.

Body

R1: Ch 2, 5 sc in second ch from hook.

R2: Sc 2 in each sc around. (10 sts)

R3: *Sc 1, 2 sc in next sc*, rep 5 times. (15 sts)

R4: *Sc 2, 2 sc in next sc*, rep 5 times. (20 sts)

R5–10: Sc 20.

Sl st 1 and fasten off, leaving long tail for sewing. Stuff and sew to head.

Arms and Legs (Make 4.)

R1: Ch 2, 6 sc in second ch from hook.

R2–7: Sc 6.

Sl st 1 and fasten off, leaving long tail for sewing. Sew open end tog and sew to body.

MOM'S HAT

Using orange yarn,

R1: Ch 2, 6 sc in second ch from hook.

R2: Sc 2 in each sc around. (12 sts)

R3: *Sc 1, 2 sc in next sc*, rep 6 times. (18 sts)

R4: *Sc 2, 2 sc in next sc*, rep 6 times. (24 sts)

R5: *Sc 3, 2 sc in next sc*, rep 6 times. (30 sts)

R6: *Sc 4, 2 sc in next sc*, rep 6 times. (36 sts)

R7: *Sc 5, 2 sc in next sc*, rep 6 times. (42 sts)

R8–16: Sc 42.

R17: Sc 8, hdc 1, dc 2, tr 2, dc 2, hdc 1, sc 13, hdc 1, dc 2, tr 2, dc 2, hdc 1, sc 5.

Change to green yarn,

R18: Sc 42.

Sl st 1 and fasten off.

Pom-pom: Make a pom-pom (see facing page) approx 1½" in diameter using green yarn and sew it on top.

Ties (make 2): Join green yarn to a sc right under one of the trebles in R17. Loosely ch 33. Starting at second ch from hook, sl st 32 and join to hat with sl st. Fasten off. Rep on other side.

FISHING POLE

Using brown for long and short branch,

Long Branch

R1: Ch 2, 5 sc in second ch from hook.

R2–23: Sc 5.

Sl st 1 and fasten off, leaving long tail for sewing. Slip pipe cleaner inside pole so it's stronger; cut off extra pipe cleaner. Sew open end tog to close it.

Little Branch

R1: Ch 2, 5 sc in second ch from hook.

R2 and 3: Sc 5.

Sl st 1 and fasten off, leaving long tail for sewing. Sew to pole.

FISH (MAKE 2.)

Use F hook and gray yarn for body and tail.

Body

R1: Ch 2, 5 sc in second ch from hook.

R2: Sc 2 in each sc around. (10 sts)

R3–5: Sc 10.

R6: Dec 5 times. (5 sts)

Sl st 1 and fasten off, leaving long tail for sewing. Sew open end tog.

Tail (Make 4.)

Ch 6, dc 1 in third ch from hook, hdc 1, sc 1, sl st 1, rep once.

Sl st 1 and fasten off. Sew 2 tails to each body.

FINISHING

First fish: Sew to baby's arms.

Second fish: Cut piece of orange yarn (as long as you want the line), knot one end to end of pole, and sew other end to fish's mouth.

Mom polar bear eye

POM-POM

1. Cut two circles from cardboard, 1½" in diameter. Cut hole in center of each circle, about ¾" in diameter. Thread long piece of yarn through tapestry needle. Hold two circles together, insert needle into hole, wrap it around, and then back through hole. Repeat, working evenly around circle, rethreading needle when necessary until circle is filled completely. When you think you have it full enough, add some more. The fuller, the better!

2. Use sharp scissors to cut yarn around edge between two pieces of cardboard.

3. Cut 12"-long piece of yarn. Run this yarn between two circles and tie very tightly. Slide circles off pom-pom and fluff it out, trimming any stray ends.

GARDEN FRIENDS:
SNAKE, MOUSE, AND BIRD

Some months ago we moved to a house after living in apartments for the longest time. Now we get to play outside more and have garden friends. Thankfully we haven't seen any snakes or mice, but lots of cute birds visit our backyard every morning!

FINISHED SIZES

Snake: Approx 12½" long
Mouse: Approx 3" long
Bird on stump: Approx 4" tall

MATERIALS

Worsted-weight yarn in red, brown, green, light pink, dark pink, and gray

Size G/6 (4 mm), F/5 (3.75 mm), and E/4 (3.5 mm) crochet hooks

6 and 9 mm plastic eyes with safety backings

Small pieces of pink and tan craft felt

Sewing thread and sharp needle

Black and pink embroidery floss and embroidery needle

Tapestry needle

Fiberfill or stuffing of your choice

Snake

Using G hook and green yarn,

Head

R1: Ch 2, 6 sc in second ch from hook.
R2: Sc 2 in each sc around. (12 sts)
R3: *Sc 1, 2 sc in next sc*, rep 6 times. (18 sts)
R4: *Sc 2, 2 sc in next sc*, rep 6 times. (24 sts)
R5–10: Sc 24.
R11: *Sc 2, dec 1*, rep 6 times. (18 sts)
Work on face: Position and attach 9 mm eyes; embroider mouth with black embroidery floss. For tongue, use the pattern on page 19 to cut snake tongue from pink felt and sew below mouth.
R12: *Sc 1, dec 1*, rep 6 times. (12 sts)
Stuff head.
R13: Dec 6 times. (6 sts)
Sl st 1 and fasten off, leaving long tail for sewing, and set aside.

Body

Using green yarn,

R1: Ch 2, 4 sc in second ch from hook.
R2: Sc 4.
R3: Sc 2 in each sc around. (8 sc)
R4: Sc 8.
Change to dark pink yarn,
R5: Sc 8.
From now on, alternate 4 rows of green and 1 row of pink (ending with 4 rows of green).

R6–59: Sc 8, stuffing very lightly as you go.

Sl st 1 and fasten off, leaving long tail for sewing. Sew body to head.

MOUSE

Start crocheting the little mouse at the nose.

Body

Using F hook and gray yarn,

R1: Ch 2, 5 sc in second ch from hook.

R2: Sc 2 in each sc around. (10 sts)

R3: Sc 10.

R4: *Sc 1, 2 sc in next sc*, rep 5 times. (15 sts)

R5: Sc 15.

R6: *Sc 2, 2 sc in next sc*, rep 5 times. (20 sts)

R7: Sc 20.

R8: *Sc 3, 2 sc in next sc*, rep 5 times. (25 sts)

Work on face: Position and attach 6 mm eyes. Embroider nose with pink embroidery floss and mouth with black embroidery floss.

R9–15: Sc 25.

R16: *Sc 3, dec 1*, rep 5 times. (20 sts)

R17: *Sc 2, dec 1*, rep 5 times. (15 sts)

R18: Sc 15.

R19: *Sc 1, dec 1*, rep 5 times. (10 sts)

Stuff.

R20: Dec 5 times. (5 sts)

Fasten off.

Ears (Make 2.)

Using F hook and gray yarn,

Ch 2, 8 sc in second ch from hook.

Fasten off, leaving long tail for sewing. Sew to body.

Front Legs (Make 2.)

Using E hook and light pink yarn,

R1: Ch 2, 4 sc in second ch from hook.

R2–4: Sc 4.

Sl st 1 and fasten off, leaving long tail for sewing. Sew open end tog and sew to body.

Back Legs (Make 2.)

Using E hook and light pink yarn,

R1: Ch 2, 6 sc in second ch from hook.

R2–4: Sc 6.

Sl st 1 and fasten off, leaving long tail for sewing. Sew to body.

Tail

Using F hook and light pink yarn,

Loosely ch 25, and starting in second ch from hook, sl st 24.

Fasten off, leaving long tail for sewing. Sew to body.

BIRD

Use F hook and red yarn throughout for Bird.

Head

R1: Ch 2, 6 sc in second ch from hook.

R2: Sc 2 in each sc. (12 sts)

R3: *Sc 1, 2 sc in next sc*, rep 6 times. (18 sts)

R4: *Sc 2, 2 sc in next sc*, rep 6 times. (24 sts)

R5–10: Sc 24.

R11: *Sc 2, dec 1*, rep 6 times. (18 sts)

Work on face: Position and attach 6 mm eyes. For beak, use the pattern on facing page to cut bird beak from tan felt, fold in half, and sew to face.

R12: *Sc 1, dec 1*, rep 6 times. (12 sts)

Stuff head firmly.

R13: Dec 6 times. (6 sts)

Fasten off and set aside.

Body

R1: Ch 2, 6 sc in second ch from hook.

R2: Sc 2 in each sc around. (12 sts)

R3: *Sc 1, 2 sc in next sc*, rep 6 times. (18 sts)

R4–7: Sc 18.

Sl st 1 and fasten off, leaving long tail for sewing. Stuff firmly and sew to head.

Wings (Make 2.)

R1: Ch 2, 5 sc in second ch from hook.

R2: Sc 2 in each sc around. (10 sts)

R3–8: Sc 10.

R9: Dec 5 times. (5 sts)

Sl st 1 and fasten off, leaving long tail for sewing. Sew open end tog and sew to body.

Tail (Make 2.)

R1: Ch 2, 6 sc in second ch from hook.

R2–8: Sc 6.

Sl st 1 and fasten off, leaving long tail for sewing. Sew to body.

Stump

Using F hook and brown yarn,

R1: Ch 2, 6 sc in second ch from hook.

R2: Sc 2 in each sc around. (12 sts)

R3: *Sc 1, 2 sc in next sc*, rep 6 times. (18 sts)

R4: *Sc 2, 2 sc in next sc*, rep 6 times. (24 sts)

R5: *Sc 3, 2 sc in next sc*, rep 6 times. (30 sts)

R6: *Sc 4, 2 sc in next sc*, rep 6 times. (36 sts)

R7: Sc 36 through back loops only.

R8–14: Sc 36.

R15: *Sc 5, 2 sc in next sc*, rep 6 times. (42 sts)

R16: Through back loops only, *sc 5, dec 1*, rep 6 times. (36 sts)

R17: *Sc 4, dec 1*, rep 6 times. (30 sts)

R18: *Sc 3, dec 1*, rep 6 times. (24 sts)

R19: *Sc 2, dec 1*, rep 6 times. (18 sts)

Stuff.

R20: *Sc 1, dec 1*, rep 6 times. (12 sts)

R21: *Sk 1 sc, sc 1*, rep 6 times. (6 sts)

Fasten off.

Little Branch

Using F hook and brown yarn,

R1: Ch 2, 4 sc in second ch from hook.

R2: Sc 2 in each sc. (8 sts)

R3 and 4: Sc 8.

Sl st 1 and fasten off, leaving long tail for sewing. Stuff and sew to stump.

Leaf

Using F hook and green yarn, loosely ch 5. Starting at second ch from hook, sl st 1, dc 2, sl st 1.

Fasten off, leaving long tail for sewing. Sew to branch.

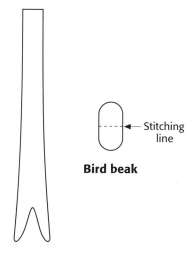

Stitching line ← (Bird beak)

Bird beak

Snake tongue

LITTLE BUNNY
AND HER CARROT HOME

Wouldn't you love to be surrounded by your favorite
food? I imagine myself in a big room full of *dulce de leche* . . . and the
ideal home for a little bunny would definitely be a carrot! This would
make a really cute Easter present; fill the carrot with jelly beans
and sit the bunny on top for a super-sweet surprise.

FINISHED SIZES

Bunny: Approx 3" tall
Carrot: Approx 7" long when closed

MATERIALS

Worsted-weight yarn in orange, green,
  and white
Size F/5 (3.75 mm) crochet hook
6 mm plastic eyes with safety backings
Pink embroidery floss and embroidery
  needle
Tapestry needle
Fiberfill or stuffing of your choice

CARROT

Top

Using orange yarn,
R1: Sc 2, 6 sc in second ch from hook.
R2: Sc 2 in every sc around. (12 sts)

R3: *Sc 1, 2 sc in next sc*, rep 6 times.
  (18 sts)
R4: *Sc 2, 2 sc in next sc*, rep 6 times.
  (24 sts)
R5: *Sc 3, 2 sc in next sc*, rep 6 times.
  (30 sts)
R6: *Sc 4, 2 sc in next sc*, rep 6 times.
  (36 sts)
R7: *Sc 5, 2 sc in next sc*, rep 6 times.
  (42 sts)
R8: *Sc 6, 2 sc in next sc*, rep 6 times.
  (48 sts)
R9–15: Sc 48.
R16: *Sc 6, dec 1*, rep 6 times. (42 sts)
R17: BPsc 42.
R18: Sc 42.
Sl st 1 and fasten off.

Bottom

Using orange yarn,
R1: Sc 2, 6 sc in second ch from hook.

R2: Sc 2 in every sc around. (12 sts)
R3: *Sc 1, 2 sc in next sc*, rep 6 times.
  (18 sts)
R4–6: Sc 18.
R7: *Sc 2, 2 sc in next sc*, rep 6 times.
  (24 sts)
R8–10: Sc 24.
R11: *Sc 3, 2 sc in next sc*, rep 6 times.
  (30 sts)
R12–14: Sc 30.
R15: *Sc 4, 2 sc in next sc*, rep 6 times.
  (36 sts)
R16–20: Sc 36.
R21: *Sc 5, 2 sc in next sc*, rep 6 times.
  (42 sts)
R22–26: Sc 42.
R27: *Sc 6, 2 sc in next sc*, rep 6 times.
  (48 sts)
R28–32: Sc 48.
Sl st 1 and fasten off.

Leaves (Make 6.)

Using green yarn,

Loosely ch 14. Starting at third ch from hook, 11 hdc, 5 hdc in next ch. You are now on other side of ch (just below what you just crocheted), 12 hdc.

Fasten off, leaving long tail for sewing. Sew to top of carrot as shown below.

LiTTLE BUNNY

Using white yarn,

Head

R1: Ch 2, 6 sc in second ch from hook.

R2: Sc 2 in each sc around. (12 sts)

R3: *Sc 1, 2 sc in next sc*, rep 6 times. (18 sts)

R4: *Sc 2, 2 sc in next sc*, rep 6 times. (24 sts)

R5–11: Sc 24.

R12: *Sc 2, dec 1*, rep 6 times. (18 sts)

Work on face: Position and attach eyes; embroider mouth and nose.

R13: *Sc 1, dec 1*, rep 6 times. (12 sts) Stuff.

R14: *Sk 1 sc, sc 1*, rep 6 times. (6 sts) Fasten off.

Ears (Make 2.)

R1: Ch 2, 6 sc in second ch from hook.

R2–4: Sc 6.

Sl st 1 and fasten off, leaving long tail for sewing. Sew to top of head.

Body

R1: Ch 2, 6 sc in second ch from hook.

R2: Sc 2 in each sc around. (12 sts)

R3: *Sc 1, 2 sc in next sc*, rep 6 times. (18 sts)

R4–8: Sc 18.

Sl st 1 and fasten off, leaving long tail for sewing. Stuff and sew to head.

Legs and Arms (Make 4.)

R1: Ch 2, 5 sc in second ch from hook.

R2–4: Sc 5.

Sl st 1 and fasten off, leaving long tail for sewing. Sew open end tog and sew to body.

Sea Friends:
Jellyfish, Cuttlefish, Dolphin, and Little Narwhal

I've been watching cartoons with the girls for a while now. I used to like them a lot (even before the girls were born), but now I'm pretty much done with their little voices and happy speech. There, I said it: I don't like cartoons anymore! To my surprise, however, there came *Ponyo*, and I fell in love. It has to be one of the sweetest, most beautiful animated movies for kids (and adults!) on the planet. We've seen it lots of times, and the sea theme just kept coming to my mind while planning this book. I think I could have made a whole book just with ocean-inspired toys.

Finished Sizes

Jellyfish: Approx 10" long including tentacles

Cuttlefish: Approx 5" long

Dolphin: Approx 7½" long

Narwhal: Approx 7" long

Materials

Worsted-weight yarn in pink, blue, gray, and white

Size G/6 (4 mm) and F/5 (3.75 mm) crochet hooks (F hook is used only for narwhal's tusk)

9 and 12 mm plastic eyes with safety backings

Black embroidery floss and embroidery needle

Tapestry needle

Fiberfill or stuffing of your choice

Jellyfish

Using G hook and pink yarn,

Body

R1: Ch 2, 6 sc in second ch from hook.

R2: Sc 2 in each sc around. (12 sts)

R3: *Sc 1, 2 sc in next sc*, rep 6 times. (18 sts)

R4: *Sc 2, 2 sc in next sc*, rep 6 times. (24 sts)

R5 and 6: Sc 24.

R7: *Sc 3, 2 sc in next sc*, rep 6 times. (30 sts)

R8: Sc 30.

R9: *Sc 4, 2 sc in next sc*, rep 6 times. (36 sts)

R10: *Sc 5, 2 sc in next sc*, rep 6 times. (42 sts)

R11–18: Sc 42.

R19: Sc 42 through back loops only (you'll use front loops later when crocheting the wavy, skirt-looking thing).

Work on face: Position and attach 12 mm eyes; embroider mouth.

R20: *Sc 5, dec 1*, rep 6 times. (36 sts)

R21: *Sc 4, dec 1*, rep 6 times. (30 sts)

R22: *Sc 3, dec 1*, rep 6 times. (24 sts)

R23: *Sc 2, dec 1*, rep 6 times. (18 sts)

R24: *Sc 1, dec 1*, rep 6 times. (12 sts)

Stuff firmly.

R25: Dec 6 times. (6 sts)

Fasten off, leaving long tail to close 6-st hole.

Wavy, Skirt-Looking Thing

Holding body upside down and starting at back, join yarn to one of the front loops you left in R19, then *hdc 4 in next st, sk 1 st, sl st 1*, rep from * to * all around body. Fasten off.

Tentacles

Inner tentacles (make 3): Loosely ch 42. Starting at third ch from hook, hdc 40. Fasten off, leaving long tail for sewing. When you have all 3, sew them tog, and then sew them to middle of bottom of body.

Outer tentacles (make 6): Loosely ch 37. Starting at second ch from hook, *sc 2, sk 1 st, sc 2, sc 3 in next st*, rep from * to *. Fasten off, leaving long tail for sewing. Sew outer tentacles to bottom, spacing them evenly around inner tentacles.

CUTTLEFISH

Use G hook.

Eye Roundies (Make 2.)

Using white yarn,

R1: Ch 2, 6 sc in second ch from hook.

R2: Sc 2 in each sc around. (12 sts)

Sl st 1 and fasten off, leaving long tail for sewing. Put 12 mm eye through middle hole and set aside.

Body

Using blue yarn,

R1: Ch 2, 6 sc in second ch from hook.

R2: Sc 2 in each sc around. (12 sts)

R3: *Sc 1, 2 sc in next sc*, rep 6 times. (18 sts)

R4: Sc 18.

R5: *Sc 2, 2 sc in next sc*, rep 6 times. (24 sts)

R6: Sc 24.

R7: *Sc 3, 2 sc in next sc*, rep 6 times. (30 sts)

R8 and 9: Sc 30.

R10: *Sc 4, 2 sc in next sc*, rep 6 times. (36 sts)

R11–22: Sc 36.

Sl st 1 and fasten off.

Work on face: Position and attach eyes (with eye roundies), sew eye roundies in place, and embroider mouth.

Base

Using blue yarn,

R1: Ch 2, 6 sc in second ch from hook.

R2: Sc 2 in each sc around. (12 sts)

R3: *Sc 1, 2 sc in next sc*, rep 6 times. (18 sts)

R4: *Sc 2, 2 sc in next sc*, rep 6 times. (24 sts)

R5: *Sc 3, 2 sc in next sc*, rep 6 times. (30 sts)

R6: *Sc 4, 2 sc in next sc*, rep 6 times. (36 sts)

Sl st 1 and fasten off, leaving long tail for sewing. Stuff body and sew base to top to close up the body.

Legs (Make 8.)

Using blue yarn,

R1: Ch 2, 4 sc in second ch from hook.

R2: Sc 2 in each sc around. (8 sts)

R3–6: Sc 8.

Sl st 1 and fasten off, leaving long tail for sewing. Stuff and sew to base as shown below.

Snout

Using gray yarn,

R1: Ch 2, 5 sc in second ch from hook.

R2: Sc 2 in each sc around. (10 sts)

R3: Sc 10.

R4: *Sc 1, 2 sc in next sc*, rep 5 times. (15 sts)

R5–7: Sc 15.

Sl st 1 and fasten off, leaving long tail for sewing. Embroider line around edge of snout (for dolphin's mouth). Stuff lightly and set aside.

Body

Using gray yarn,

R1: Ch 2, 5 sc in second ch from hook.

R2: Sc 2 in each sc around. (10 sts)

R3: *Sc 1, 2 sc in next sc*, rep 5 times. (15 sts)

R4: *Sc 2, 2 sc in next sc*, rep 5 times. (20 sts)

R5: *Sc 3, 2 sc in next sc*, rep 5 times. (25 sts)

R6: *Sc 4, 2 sc in next sc*, rep 5 times. (30 sts)

R7: *Sc 5, 2 sc in next sc*, rep 5 times. (35 sts)

R8–11: Sc 35.

R12: *Sc 5, dec 1*, rep 5 times. (30 sts)

R13–16: Sc 30.

Work on face: Position and attach eyes (with eye roundies); sew roundies in place. Flatten snout and sew to face.

R17 and 18: Sc 30.

R19: *Sc 4, dec 1*, rep 5 times. (25 sts)

DOLPHIN

Using G hook,

Eye Roundies (Make 2.)

Using blue yarn,

R1: Ch 2, 5 sc in second ch from hook.

R2: Sc 2 in each sc around. (10 sts)

R3: *Sc 1, 2 sc in next sc*, rep 5 times. (15 sts)

R4: *Sc 2, 2 sc in next sc*, rep 5 times. (20 sts)

Sl st 1 and fasten off, leaving long tail for sewing. Put 12 mm eye through middle hole and set aside.

R20 and 21: Sc 25.

R22: *Sc 3, dec 1*, rep 5 times. (20 sts)

R23–26: Sc 20.

R27: *Sc 2, dec 1*, rep 5 times. (15 sts)

R28: Sc 15.

Stuff firmly.

R29: *Sc 1, dec 1*, rep 5 times. (10 sts)

R30: Dec 5 times.

Sl st 1 and fasten off.

Pectoral Flippers (Make 2.)

Using gray yarn,

R1: Ch 2, 6 sc in second ch from hook.

R2: Sc 6.

R3: Sc 2 in each sc around. (12 sts)

R4–6: Sc 12.

Sl st 1 and fasten off, leaving long tail for sewing. Sew open end tog and sew to sides of body.

Dorsal Fin

Using gray yarn,

R1: Ch 2, 5 sc in second ch from hook.

R2: Sc 5.

R3: Sc 2 in each sc around. (10 sts)

R4 and 5: Sc 10.

Sl st 1 and fasten off, leaving long tail for
  sewing. Sew to top of body.

Tail (Make 2.)

Using gray yarn,

R1: Ch 2, 5 sc in second ch from hook.

R2: Sc 5.

R3: Sc 2 in each sc around. (10 sts)

R4–7: Sc 10.

R8: Dec 5 times. (5 sts)

Sl st 1 and fasten off, leaving long tail for
  sewing. Sew to body.

LiTTLe NaRWHaL

Use G hook, except for tusk.

Eye Roundies (Make 2.)

Using white yarn,

R1: Ch 2, 6 sc in second ch from hook.

R2: Sc 2 in each sc around. (12 sts)

Sl st 1 and fasten off, leaving long tail for
  sewing. Put 9 mm eye through middle
  hole and set aside.

Body

Using blue yarn,

R1: Ch 2, 5 sc in second ch from hook.

R2: Sc 2 in each sc around. (10 sts)

R3: *Sc 1, 2 sc in next sc*, rep 5 times.
  (15 sts)

R4: *Sc 2, 2 sc in next sc*, rep 5 times.
  (20 sts)

R5: *Sc 3, 2 sc in next sc*, rep 5 times.
  (25 sts)

R6–12: Sc 25.

Work on face: Position and attach eyes
  (with eye roundies); sew eye roundies
  in place. Embroider mouth.

R13: *Sc 3, dec 1*, rep 5 times. (20 sts)

R14–16: Sc 20.

R17–21: *Sc 2, dec 1*, rep 5 times. (15 sts)

Stuff almost to top.

R22: *Sc 1, dec 1*, rep 5 times. (10 sts)

R23: Sc 10.

R24: *Sk 1 sc, sc 1*, rep 5 times. (5 sts)

Sl st 1 and fasten off.

Flippers (Make 2.)

Using blue yarn,

R1: Ch 2, 5 sc in second ch from hook.

R2: Sc 5.

R3: Sc 2 in each sc around. (10 sts)

R4 and 5: Sc 10.

Sl st 1 and fasten off, leaving long tail for
  sewing. Sew open end tog and sew
  to sides of body.

Tail (Make 2.)

Using blue yarn,

R1: Ch 2, 5 sc in second ch from hook.

R2: Sc 5.

R3: Sc 2 in each sc around. (10 sts)

R4–6: Sc 10.

R7: Dec 5 times. (5 sts)

Sl st 1 and fasten off, leaving long tail for
  sewing. Sew open end tog and sew
  to body.

Tusk

Using F hook and white yarn,

R1: Ch 2, 4 sc in second ch from hook.

R2: Sc 4.

R3: Sc 2 in each sc around. (8 sts)

R4–9: Sc 8, stuffing as you go.

Sl st 1 and fasten off, leaving long tail for
  sewing. Sew to face.

SANTIAGO, MY LITTLE BOSTON TERRIER

Santiago is my first dog ever. I'd
been wanting a dog for as long as I can remember.
We got him when he was a little over two months, and now he just
turned two. Franco, my husband, wasn't too keen about it at first, but here
he is, and we all adore him. I never thought you could love a dog so much!
I'm learning how to take care of him, little by little. He went to the vet way too
many times the first year of his life (I know what to do with baby humans, but
I had no idea what to do with Santiago). I'm amazed at how smart and
loving he is; you should see him with Martina. So now I think he deserves
a little Boston friend, and I'm working on it—although Franco's been
a lot clearer in saying "I don't think so" since Santi came
into our lives. Wish me luck!

FINISHED SIZES

Boston terrier: Approx 5" tall
Bed: Approx 4½" diameter

MATERIALS

Worsted-weight yarn in black, white, and red

Size G/6 (4 mm) crochet hook

12 mm plastic eyes with safety backings

Black embroidery floss and embroidery needle

Tapestry needle

Fiberfill or stuffing of your choice

SANTIAGO

Muzzle

Using white yarn,

R1: Ch 2, 6 sc in second ch from hook.

R2: Sc 2 in each sc around. (12 sts)

R3: *Sc 1, 2 sc in next sc*, rep 6 times. (18 sts)

R4 and 5: Sc 18.

Sl st 1 and fasten off, leaving long tail for sewing. Embroider nose and mouth and set aside.

Stripe Above Muzzle

Using white yarn and working back and forth, loosely ch 4.

R1: Sc 3, starting in second ch from hook.

R2 and 3: Ch 1, sc 3, turn.

R4: Ch 1, 2 sc in next sc, sc 1, 2 sc in next sc, turn. (5 sts)

R5: Ch 1, sc 5.

Fasten off, leaving long tail for sewing, and set aside.

Head

Using black yarn,

R1: Ch 2, 7 sc in second ch from hook.

R2: Sc 2 in each sc around. (14 sts)

R3: *Sc 1, 2 sc in next sc*, rep 7 times. (21 sts)

R4: *Sc 2, 2 sc in next sc*, rep 7 times. (28 sts)

R5: *Sc 3, 2 sc in next sc*, rep 7 times. (35 sts)

R6–14: Sc 35.

R15: *Sc 3, dec 1*, rep 7 times. (28 sts)

R16 and 17: Sc 28.

Work on face: Stuff muzzle a little and sew to face. Sew white stripe to head (making sure wider end is at top). Position and attach eyes.

R18: *Sc 2, dec 1*, rep 7 times. (21 sts)

R19: *Sc 1, dec 1*, rep 7 times. (14 sts)

Stuff firmly.

R20: Dec 7 times. (7 sts)

Fasten off.

Ears (Make 2.)

Using black yarn,

R1: Ch 2, 4 sc in second ch from hook.

R2: Sc 2 in each sc around. (8 sts)

R3: Sc 8.

R4: *Sc 1, 2 sc in next sc*, rep 4 times. (12 sts)

R5–8: Sc 12.

Sl st 1 and fasten off, leaving long tail for sewing. Sew to head.

Body

Using black yarn,

R1: Ch 2, 7 sc in second ch from hook.

R2: Sc 2 in each sc around. (14 sts)

R3: *Sc 1, 2 sc in next sc*, rep 7 times. (21 sts)

R4–8: Sc 21.

Change to white yarn,

R9–11: Sc 21.

Sl st 1 and fasten off, leaving long tail for sewing. Stuff and sew to head.

Legs (Make 4.)

Using black for back legs and white for front legs,

R1: Ch 2, 5 sc in second ch from hook.

R2: Sc 2 in each sc around. (10 sts)

R3–5: Sc 10.

Change to black if you started with white for front legs, or cont with black if you're making back legs.

R6–10: Sc 10.

Sl st 1 and fasten off, leaving long tail for sewing. Stuff lightly, sew open end tog, and sew to body.

BED AND PILLOW

Bed

Using red yarn,

R1: Ch 2, 5 sc in second ch from hook.

R2: Sc 2 in each sc around. (10 sts)

R3: *Sc 1, 2 sc in next sc*, rep 5 times. (15 sts)

R4: *Sc 2, 2 sc in next sc*, rep 5 times. (20 sts)

R5: *Sc 3, 2 sc in next sc*, rep 5 times. (25 sts)

R6: *Sc 4, 2 sc in next sc*, rep 5 times. (30 sts)

R7: *Sc 5, 2 sc in next sc*, rep 5 times. (35 sts)

R8: *Sc 6, 2 sc in next sc*, rep 5 times. (40 sts)

R9: *Sc 7, 2 sc in next sc*, rep 5 times. (45 sts)

R10: *Sc 8, 2 sc in next sc*, rep 5 times. (50 sts)

R11: *Sc 9, 2 sc in next sc*, rep 5 times. (55 sts)

R12: *Sc 10, 2 sc in next sc*, rep 5 times. (60 sts)

R13: Sc 60.

R14: Sc 60 through back loops only.

R15–21: Sc 60.

Sl st 1 and fasten off.

Pillow

Rep instructions for the bed through R11.

R12: Sc 55.

Sl st 1 and fasten off.

Make another circle for other side of pillow. With WS tog, align sts of 2 circles, sew approx ¾ of the way around, stuff lightly, and finish sewing. Let your puppy take a nap!

MOM AND BABY DUCK

I love to see baby ducks and their moms walking in a line, and I think they would look extra cute with little hats on, especially bear and apple ones!

FINISHED SIZES

Mom duck: Approx 5" tall
Baby duck: Approx 3½" tall

MATERIALS

Worsted-weight yarn in white, yellow, orange, red, brown, and green

Size G/6 (4 mm) crochet hook

9 and 12 mm plastic eyes with safety backings

Tapestry needle

Fiberfill or stuffing of your choice

MOM DUCK

Beak

Using orange yarn,

R1: Ch 2, 7 sc in second ch from hook.

R2: Sc 2 in each sc around. (14 sts)

R3–5: Sc 14.

Sl st 1 and fasten off, leaving long tail for sewing, and set aside.

Head

Using white yarn,

R1: Ch 2, 6 sc in second ch from hook.

R2: Sc 2 in each sc around. (12 sts)

R3: *Sc 1, 2 sc in next sc*, rep 6 times. (18 sts)

R4: *Sc 2, 2 sc in next sc*, rep 6 times. (24 sts)

R5: *Sc 3, 2 sc in next sc*, rep 6 times. (30 sts)

R6: *Sc 4, 2 sc in next sc*, rep 6 times. (36 sts)

R7: *Sc 5, 2 sc in next sc*, rep 6 times. (42 sts)

R8–16: Sc 42.

R17: *Sc 5, dec 1*, rep 6 times. (36 sts)

R18: *Sc 4, dec 1*, rep 6 times. (30 sts)

R19: *Sc 3, dec 1*, rep 6 times. (24 sts)

R20: Sc 24.

Work on face: Sew beak in place; position and attach 12 mm eyes.

R21: *Sc 2, dec 1*, rep 6 times. (18 sts)

R22: *Sc 1, dec 1*, rep 6 times. (12 sts)

Stuff head firmly.

R23: *Sk 1 sc, sc 1*, rep 6 times. (6 sts)

Fasten off.

Body

Using white yarn,

R1: Ch 2, 5 sc in second ch from hook.

R2: Sc 2 in each sc around. (10 sts)

R3: *Sc 1, 2 sc in next sc*, rep 5 times. (15 sts)

R4: *Sc 2, 2 sc in next sc*, rep 5 times. (20 sts)

R5: *Sc 3, 2 sc in next sc*, rep 5 times. (25 sts)

R6–13: Sc 25.

Sl st 1 and fasten off, leaving long tail for sewing. Stuff and sew to head.

Wings (Make 2.)

Using white yarn,

R1: Ch 2, 5 sc in second ch from hook.

R2: Sc 2 in each sc around. (10 sts)

R3: *Sc 1, 2 sc in next sc*, rep 5 times. (15 sts)

R4–7: Sc 15.

Sl st 1 and fasten off, leaving long tail for sewing. Sew open end tog and sew to body.

Feet (Make 2.)

Using orange yarn,

R1: Ch 2, 7 sc in second ch from hook.

R2: Sc 2 in each sc around. (14 sts)

R3–7: Sc 14.

Sl st 1 and fasten off, leaving long tail for sewing. Sew open end tog and sew to body.

Mom's Apple Hat

Using red yarn,

R1: Ch 2, 6 sc in second ch from hook.

R2: Sc 2 in each sc around. (12 sts)

R3: *Sc 1, 2 sc in next sc*, rep 6 times. (18 sts)

R4: *Sc 2, 2 sc in next sc*, rep 6 times. (24 sts)

R5: *Sc 3, 2 sc in next sc*, rep 6 times. (30 sts)

R6: *Sc 4, 2 sc in next sc*, rep 6 times. (36 sts)

R7: *Sc 5, 2 sc in next sc*, rep 6 times. (42 sts)

R8: *Sc 6, 2 sc in next sc*, rep 6 times. (48 sts)

R9–15: Sc 48.

Sl st 1 and fasten off.

Stem: Using brown yarn, loosely ch 5. Starting at second ch from hook, sl st 4. Fasten off, leaving long tail for sewing. Sew to hat.

Leaf: Using green yarn, loosely ch 10. Starting at second ch from hook, sl st 1, hdc 1, dc 1, tr 3, dc 1, hdc 1, sl st 1. Fasten off, leaving long tail for sewing. Sew leaf next to stem.

BABY DUCK

Beak

Using orange yarn,

R1: Ch 2, 5 sc in second ch from hook.

R2: Sc 2 in each sc around. (10 sts)

R3: Sc 10.

Sl st 1 and fasten off, leaving long tail for sewing, and set aside.

Head

Using yellow yarn,

R1: Ch 2, 6 sc in second ch from hook.

R2: Sc 2 in each sc around. (12 sts)

R3: *Sc 1, 2 sc in next sc*, rep 6 times. (18 sts)

R4: *Sc 2, 2 sc in next sc*, rep 6 times. (24 sts)

R5: *Sc 3, 2 sc in next sc*, rep 6 times. (30 sts)

R6–12: Sc 30.

R13: *Sc 3, dec 1*, rep 6 times. (24 sts)

R14: *Sc 2, dec 1*, rep 6 times. (18 sts)

R15: Sc 18.

Work on face: Sew beak in place; position and attach 9 mm eyes.

R16: *Sc 1, dec 1*, rep 6 times. (12 sts) Stuff head firmly.

R17: *Sk 1 sc, sc 1*, rep 6 times. (6 sts) Fasten off.

Body

Using yellow yarn,

R1: Ch 2, 6 sc in second ch from hook.

R2: Sc 2 in each sc around. (12 sts)

R3: *Sc 1, 2 sc in next sc*, rep 6 times. (18 sts)

R4–9: Sc 18.

Fasten off, leaving long tail for sewing. Stuff and sew to head.

Wings (Make 2.)

Using yellow yarn,

R1: Ch 2, 4 sc in second ch from hook.

R2: Sc 2 in each sc around. (8 sts)

R3–5: Sc 8.

Sl st 1 and fasten off, leaving long tail for sewing. Sew open end tog and sew to body.

Feet (Make 2.)

Using orange yarn,

R1: Ch 2, 5 sc in second ch from hook.

R2: Sc 2 in each sc around. (10 sts)

R3–5: Sc 10.

Sl st 1 and fasten off, leaving long tail for sewing. Sew open end tog and sew to body.

Baby's Bear Hat

Using brown yarn,

R1: Ch 2, 6 sc in second ch from hook.

R2: Sc 2 in each sc around. (12 sts)

R3: *Sc 1, 2 sc in next sc*, rep 6 times. (18 sts)

R4: *Sc 2, 2 sc in next sc*, rep 6 times. (24 sts)

R5: *Sc 3, 2 sc in next sc*, rep 6 times. (30 sts)

R6: *Sc 4, 2 sc in next sc*, rep 6 times. (36 sts)

R7–10: Sc 36.

Sl st 1 and fasten off.

Ears (make 2): Ch 2, 8 sc in second ch from hook. Fasten off, leaving long tail for sewing. Sew to hat.

LittLe Pig and MOM

When Oli was little she really liked pigs. I think it's because she also really liked everything and anything that was pink. She slept with a little stuffed piggy for years. Then the pig disappeared for a while (everything disappears in our house, especially since Martina started walking), but a couple of months ago Marti found it and Oli was so happy! It just seemed fitting to update the little pig and give him a mom and a little vest. Although Oli really liked them, it's the old piggy that's back to sleeping with her after all these years.

FINISHED SIZES

Mom pig: Approx 7" tall
Little pig: Approx 4½" tall

MATERIALS

Worsted-weight yarn in pink, red, white, and tan

Size G/6 (4 mm) and F/5 (3.75 mm) crochet hooks

9 and 12 mm plastic eyes with safety backings

Small piece of black craft felt

Black embroidery floss and embroidery needle

Tapestry needle

Fiberfill or stuffing of your choice

MOM PIG

Use G hook.

Muzzle

Using pink yarn,

R1: Ch 2, 6 sc in second ch from hook.

R2: Sc 2 in each sc around. (12 sts)

R3: *Sc 1, 2 sc in next sc*, rep 6 times. (18 sts)

R4: Sc 18.

Sl st 1 and fasten off, leaving long tail for sewing. For nostrils, use the pattern on page 39 to cut 2 circles from black felt, sew to muzzle, and set aside.

Eye Roundies (Make 2.)

Using white yarn,

R1: Ch 2, 5 sc in second ch from hook.

R2: Sc 2 in each sc around. (10 sts)

R3: *Sc 1, 2 sc in next sc*, rep 5 times. (15 sts)

Sl st 1 and fasten off, leaving long tail for sewing. Put 12 mm eye through middle hole and set aside.

Head

Using pink yarn,

R1: Ch 2, 6 sc in second ch from hook.

R2: Sc 2 in each sc around. (12 sts)

R3: *Sc 1, 2 sc in next sc*, rep 6 times. (18 sts)

R4: *Sc 2, 2 sc in next sc*, rep 6 times. (24 sts)

R5: *Sc 3, 2 sc in next sc*, rep 6 times. (30 sts)

R6: *Sc 4, 2 sc in next sc*, rep 6 times. (36 sts)

R7: *Sc 5, 2 sc in next sc*, rep 6 times. (42 sts)

R8–17: Sc 42.

R18: *Sc 5, dec 1*, rep 6 times. (36 sts)

R19: *Sc 4, dec 1*, rep 6 times. (30 sts)

R20: *Sc 3, dec 1*, rep 6 times. (24 sts)

R21: Sc 24.

Work on face: Stuff muzzle a little and sew to face. Position and attach eyes (with eye roundies); sew eye roundies in place.

R22: *Sc 2, dec 1*, rep 6 times. (18 sts)

R23: *Sc 1, dec 1*, rep 6 times. (12 sts)

Stuff head firmly.

R24: Dec 6 times. (6 sts)

Fasten off.

Ears (Make 2.)

Using pink yarn,

R1: Ch 2, 6 sc in second ch from hook.

R2: Sc 6.

R3: Sc 2 in each sc around. (12 sts)

R4 and 5: Sc 12.

Sl st 1 and fasten off, leaving long tail for sewing. Sew open end tog and sew to head.

Body

Using pink yarn,

R1: Ch 2, 5 sc in second ch from hook.

R2: Sc 2 in each sc around. (10 sts)

R3: *Sc 1, 2 sc in next sc*, rep 5 times. (15 sts)

R4: *Sc 2, 2 sc in next sc*, rep 5 times. (20 sts)

R5: *Sc 3, 2 sc in next sc*, rep 5 times. (25 sts)

R6–9: Sc 25.

Change to red and start alternating 1 row with red and 1 row with white until the end.

R10–16: Sc 25.

Sl st 1 and fasten off, leaving long tail for sewing. Stuff and sew to head.

Arms and Legs (Make 4.)

Using pink yarn,

R1: Ch 2, 5 sc in second ch from hook.

R2: Sc 2 in each sc around. (10 sts)

R3–10: Sc 10.

Sl st 1 and fasten off, leaving long tail for sewing. Stuff, sew open end of arms tog, and sew all to body.

LITTLE PIG

Use F hook.

Muzzle

Using tan yarn,

R1: Ch 2, 6 sc in second ch from hook.

R2: Sc 2 in each sc around. (12 sts)

R3: *Sc 1, 2 sc in next sc*, rep 6 times. (18 sts)

R4: Sc 18.

Sl st 1 and fasten off, leaving long tail for sewing. For nostrils, use the pattern to cut 2 circles from black felt, sew to muzzle, and set aside.

Eye Roundies (Make 2.)

Using white yarn,

R1: Ch 2, 6 sc in second ch from hook.

R2: Sc 2 in each sc around. (12 sts)

Sl st 1 and fasten off, leaving long tail for sewing. Put 9 mm eye through middle hole and set aside.

Head

Using tan yarn,

R1: Ch 2, 6 sc in second ch from hook.

R2: Sc 2 in each sc around. (12 sts)

R3: *Sc 1, 2 sc in next sc*, rep 6 times. (18 sts)

R4: *Sc 2, 2 sc in next sc*, rep 6 times. (24 sts)

R5: *Sc 3, 2 sc in next sc*, rep 6 times. (30 sts)

R6–12: Sc 30.

R13: *Sc 3, dec 1*, rep 6 times. (24 sts)

R14: *Sc 2, dec 1*, rep 6 times. (18 sts)

R15 and 16: Sc 18.

Work on face: Stuff muzzle a little and sew to face. Position and attach eyes (with eye roundies) and sew roundies in place.

R17: *Sc 1, dec 1*, rep 6 times. (12 sts)

Stuff firmly.

R18: Dec 6 times. (6 sts)

Fasten off.

Ears (Make 2.)

Using tan yarn,

R1: Ch 2, 6 sc in second ch from hook.

R2: Sc 6.

R3: Sc 2 in each sc around. (12 sts)

R4: Sc 12.

Sl st 1 and fasten off, leaving long tail for sewing. Sew open end tog and sew to head.

Body

Using tan yarn,

R1: Ch 2, 6 sc in second ch from hook.

R2: Sc 2 in each sc around. (12 sts)

R3: *Sc 1, 2 sc in next sc*, rep 6 times. (18 sts)

R4–10: Sc 18.

Sl st 1 and fasten off, leaving long tail for sewing. Stuff and sew to head.

Arms and Legs (Make 4.)

R1: Ch 2, 6 sc in second ch from hook.

R2–5: Sc 6.

Sl st 1 and fasten off, leaving long tail for sewing. Sew open end tog of arms only; then sew all to body.

Vest

Using red yarn,

Loosely ch 23.

R1: Starting at second ch from hook, sc 22. (22 sts)

R2: Ch 1, sc 3, ch 5, sk 5 sts, sc 6, ch 5, sk 5 sts, sc 3, turn.

R3: Ch 1, sc 3, sc 5 in 5-sp ch, sc 6, sc 5 in 5-sp ch, sc 3, turn. (22 sts)

R4: Ch 1, sc 22, turn.

Fasten off.

Ties: Join yarn to one of the top corners of vest, ch 16, fasten off. Rep on opposite side.

Put vest on baby pig and secure ties at neck.

Pig nostril

Tree Love

Have you heard the saying that everyone should plant a tree in his or her lifetime? Well, I'm horrible—really horrible—at taking care of plants, so I figure planting a tree is definitely out of the question for me. Instead, I crocheted one! It makes the nicest little present for a wholehearted tree hugger.

FINISHED SIZE

Approx 6½" tall

MATERIALS

Worsted-weight yarn in brown and 2 shades of green

Size F/5 (3.75 mm) crochet hook

12 mm plastic eyes with safety backings

Black embroidery floss and embroidery needle

Tapestry needle

Poly-Pellets or rice for trunk (see sidebar)

Fiberfill or stuffing of your choice for branches

1 nylon stocking (toe end only; see sidebar)

POLY-PELLETS OR RICE

The tree will not stand up on its own when stuffed with fiberfill, so use Poly-Pellets or rice for the stuffing. To keep the pellets or rice from going through the crochet stitches, you need to put them in a nylon stocking. From the toe end of a stocking, cut a piece about 10" long. Put the pellets or rice into the stocking and check to see that it's full enough. Add more when you're close to the end if necessary. Tie a knot in the end of the stocking and stuff the end inside before you close the hole. Your pellets are now secure inside your little tree.

TRUNK

Using brown yarn,

R1: Ch 2, 6 sc in second ch from hook.

R2: Sc 2 in each sc around. (12 sts)

R3: *Sc 1, 2 sc in next sc*, rep 6 times. (18 sts)

R4: *Sc 2, 2 sc in next sc*, rep 6 times. (24 sts)

R5: *Sc 3, 2 sc in next sc*, rep 6 times. (30 sts)

R6: *Sc 4, 2 sc in next sc*, rep 6 times. (36 sts)

R7: *Sc 5, 2 sc in next sc*, rep 6 times. (42 sts)

R8–17: Sc 42.

R18: *Sc 5, dec 1*, rep 6 times. (36 sts)

R19–22: Sc 36.

Work on face: Position and attach eyes; embroider mouth.

R23–28: *Sc 4, dec 1*, rep 6 times. (30 sts)

R29–32: *Sc 3, dec 1*, rep 6 times. (24 sts)

R33: *Sc 2, dec 1*, rep 6 times. (18 sts)

R34: Sc 18.

Stuff almost to the top with Poly-Pellets or rice inside a stocking.

R35: *Sc 1, dec 1*, rep 6 times. (12 sts)

R36: Sc 12.

R37: *Sk 1 sc, sc 1*, rep 6 times. (6 sts)

Finish stuffing and tie a knot in end of stocking. Add a little bit of fiberfill. Fasten off, leaving long tail to close up 6-st hole.

LONG BRANCHES

Make as many as you want; I made 8.

Using brown yarn,

R1: Ch 2, 4 sc in second ch from hook.

R2: Sc 2 in each sc around. (8 sts)

R3–11: Sc 8, stuffing as you go.

Sl st 1 and fasten off, leaving long tail for sewing. Stuff lightly and sew to trunk, referring to photos on page 41 and below.

SHORT BRANCHES

Make as many as you want; I made 8 (1 for each long branch).

Using brown yarn,

R1: Ch 2, 6 sc in second ch from hook.

R2–4: Sc 6.

Sl st 1 and fasten off, leaving long tail for sewing. Sew to long branches.

LEAVES

Make lots using both green yarns.

Loosely ch 6. Starting at second ch from hook, sl st 1, dc 1, tr 1, dc 1, sl st 1.

Fasten off, leaving long tail for sewing. Sew to branches.

MOM AND BABY KOALA

I think koalas have to be among the sweetest-looking animals. I sewed the little baby to the mom's back, but you could attach Velcro on the baby's hands and the mom's back so the baby can be removed to go out and play!

FINISHED SIZES

Mom koala: Approx 5" tall
Baby koala: Approx 3" tall

MATERIALS

Worsted-weight yarn in gray, white, and pink

Size G/6 (4 mm) crochet hook

9 and 12 mm plastic eyes with safety backings

Small piece of black craft felt

Black embroidery floss and embroidery needle

Tapestry needle

Fiberfill or stuffing of your choice

MOM KOALA

Eye Roundies (Make 2.)

Using white yarn,

R1: Ch 2, 6 sc in second ch from hook.

R2: Sc 2 in each sc around. (12 sts)

Sl st 1 and fasten off, leaving long tail for sewing. Put 12 mm eye through middle hole and set aside.

Head

Using gray yarn,

R1: Ch 2, 5 sc in second ch from hook.

R2: Sc 2 in each sc around. (10 sts)

R3: *Sc 1, 2 sc in next sc*, rep 5 times. (15 sts)

R4: *Sc 2, 2 sc in next sc*, rep 5 times. (20 sts)

R5: *Sc 3, 2 sc in next sc*, rep 5 times. (25 sts)

R6: *Sc 4, 2 sc in next sc*, rep 5 times. (30 sts)

R7: *Sc 5, 2 sc in next sc*, rep 5 times. (35 sts)

R8: *Sc 6, 2 sc in next sc*, rep 5 times. (40 sts)

R9–17: Sc 40.

R18: *Sc 6, dec 1*, rep 5 times. (35 sts)

R19: *Sc 5, dec 1*, rep 5 times. (30 sts)

R20: Sc 30.

Work on face: Position and attach eyes (with eye roundies) and sew roundies in place. Use the pattern on page 45 to cut nose from black felt and sew in place; embroider mouth.

R21: *Sc 4, dec 1*, rep 5 times. (25 sts)

R22: *Sc 3, dec 1*, rep 5 times. (20 sts)

R23: *Sc 2, dec 1*, rep 5 times. (15 sts)

Stuff head.

R24: *Sc 1, dec 1*, rep 5 times. (10 sts)

R25: Dec 5 times. (5 sts)

Fasten off.

Ears (Make 2.)

Using gray yarn,

R1: Ch 2, 5 sc in second ch from hook.

R2: Sc 2 in each sc around. (10 sts)

R3: *Sc 1, 2 sc in next sc*, rep 5 times. (15 sts)

R4 and 5: Sc 15.

Sl st 1 and fasten off, leaving long tail for sewing. Sew open end tog and sew to head.

Body

Using gray yarn,

R1: Ch 2, 5 sc in second ch from hook.

R2: Sc 2 in each sc around. (10 sts)

R3: *Sc 1, 2 sc in next sc*, rep 5 times. (15 sts)

R4: *Sc 2, 2 sc in next sc*, rep 5 times. (20 sts)

R5: *Sc 3, 2 sc in next sc*, rep 5 times. (25 sts)

R6–14: Sc 25.

Sl st 1 and fasten off, leaving long tail for sewing. Stuff and sew to head.

Arms and Legs (Make 4.)

Using gray yarn,

R1: Ch 2, 5 sc in second ch from hook.

R2: Sc 2 in each sc around. (10 sts)

R3–9: Sc 10.

Sl st 1 and fasten off, leaving long tail for sewing. Stuff, sew open end tog, and sew to body.

BaBY KOaLa

Eye Roundies (Make 2.)

Using white yarn,

R1: Ch 2, 5 sc in second ch from hook.

R2: Sc 2 in each sc around. (10 sts)

Sl st 1 and fasten off, leaving long tail for sewing. Put 9 mm eye through middle hole and set aside.

Head

Using gray yarn,

R1: Ch 2, 5 sc in second ch from hook.

R2: Sc 2 in each sc around. (10 sts)

R3: *Sc 1, 2 sc in next sc*, rep 5 times. (15 sts)

R4: *Sc 2, 2 sc in next sc*, rep 5 times. (20 sts)

R5: *Sc 3, 2 sc in next sc*, rep 5 times. (25 sts)

R6–11: Sc 25.

R12: *Sc 3, dec 1*, rep 5 times. (20 sts)

Work on face: Position and attach eyes (with eye roundies) and sew roundies

in place. Use the pattern to cut nose from black felt and sew in place; embroider mouth.

R13: *Sc 2, dec 1*, rep 5 times. (15 sts)

R14: *Sc 1, dec 1*, rep 5 times. (10 sts)

Stuff head.

R15: Dec 5 times. (5 sts)

Fasten off.

Ears (Make 2.)

Using gray yarn,

R1: Ch 2, 5 sc in second ch from hook.

R2: Sc 2 in each sc around. (10 sts)

R3 and 4: Sc 10.

Sl st 1 and fasten off, leaving long tail for sewing. Sew to head.

Body

Using pink yarn,

R1: Ch 2, 5 sc in second ch from hook.

R2: Sc 2 in each sc around. (10 sts)

R3: *Sc 1, 2 sc in next sc*, rep 5 times. (15 sts)

R4–7: Sc 15.

Sl st 1 and fasten off, leaving long tail for sewing. Stuff and sew to head.

Arms and Legs (Make 4.)

Using gray yarn,

R1: Ch 2, 5 sc in second ch from hook.

R2–5: Sc 5.

Sl st 1 and fasten off, leaving long tail for sewing. Sew open end tog and sew to body. Sew baby's arms to mommy's neck.

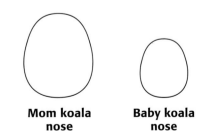

Mom koala nose   **Baby koala nose**

These happy little strawberries will make you smile every day.
They look super cute on my desk right next to the computer . . .
until Martina gets hold of them and they get the royal
treatment as her little "baby strawberries."

FINISHED SIZE

Approx 3½" tall

MATERIALS

Worsted-weight yarn in green, red, brown, and tan

Size F/5 (3.75 mm) crochet hook

6 mm plastic eyes with safety backings

Black embroidery floss and embroidery needle

Tapestry needle

Fiberfill or stuffing of your choice

POT

Using brown yarn,

R1: Ch 2, 6 sc in second ch from hook.

R2: Sc 2 in each sc around. (12 sts)

R3: *Sc 1, 2 sc in next sc*, rep 6 times. (18 sts)

R4: *Sc 2, 2 sc in next sc*, rep 6 times. (24 sts)

R5: *Sc 3, 2 sc in next sc*, rep 6 times. (30 sts)

R6: *Sc 4, 2 sc in next sc*, rep 6 times. (36 sts)

R7: *Sc 5, 2 sc in next sc*, rep 6 times. (42 sts)

R8: *Sc 6, 2 sc in next sc*, rep 6 times. (48 sts)

R9: *Sc 7, 2 sc in next sc*, rep 6 times. (54 sts)

R10: Through back loops only, *sc 7, dec 1*, rep 6 times. (48 sts)

R11–17: Sc 48.

Sl st 1 and fasten off.

DIRT

Using tan yarn,

R1: Ch 2, 6 sc in second ch from hook.

R2: Sc 2 in each sc around. (12 sts)

R3: *Sc 1, 2 sc in next sc*, rep 6 times. (18 sts)

R4: *Sc 2, 2 sc in next sc*, rep 6 times. (24 sts)

R5: *Sc 3, 2 sc in next sc*, rep 6 times. (30 sts)

R6: *Sc 4, 2 sc in next sc*, rep 6 times. (36 sts)

R7: *Sc 5, 2 sc in next sc*, rep 6 times. (42 sts)

R8: *Sc 6, 2 sc in next sc*, rep 6 times. (48 sts)

Sl st 1 and fasten off, leaving long tail for sewing; set aside.

STRAWBERRIES (Make 2.)

Using red yarn,

R1: Ch 2, 6 sc in second ch from hook.

R2: Sc 6.

R3: Sc 2 in each sc around. (12 sts)

R4–8: Sc 12.

Work on face: Position and attach eyes; embroider mouth. Stuff.

R9: Dec 6 times. (6 sts)

Fasten off.

Leaves on Strawberries (Make 2.)

Using green yarn,

R1: Ch 2, 6 sc in second ch from hook.

R2: *Ch 4, and working on that ch and beg in second ch from hook, sl st 1, sc 1, dc 1, sk 1 sc, sl st 1*, work 3 more times.

Fasten off, leaving long tail for sewing. Sew to top of strawberries.

Leaves in Pot (Make 8.)

Using green yarn,

R1: Ch 2, 6 sc in second ch from hook.

R2: Sc 2 in each sc around. (12 sts)

R3–6: Sc 12.

R7: Dec 6 times. (6 sts)

Fasten off, leaving long tail for sewing. Sew open end tog.

FiNiSHiNG

Sew leaves and strawberries to dirt. Position dirt inside of pot (approx ½" from top), and using long tail, sew approx ¾ of the way around; stuff pot and finish sewing.

LITTLE KITTEN AND BED

Oli's allergic to cats, so this is the closest she can get to one without her eyes turning all puffy and scary looking. When she was little, my friends would ask her if she had any allergies before giving her a snack, and she would say "Cats." My friends used to tease me, saying it sounded like we actually fed her cats!

FINISHED SIZES

Little kitten: Approx 4" long not including tail

Bed: Approx 4½" diameter

MATERIALS

Worsted-weight yarn in tan, white, and yellow (plus scrap for yarn ball)

Size F/5 (3.75 mm) and G/6 (4 mm) crochet hooks

9 mm plastic eyes with safety backings

Black embroidery floss and embroidery needle

Tapestry needle

Fiberfill or stuffing of your choice

LITTLE KITTEN

Use F hook.

Muzzle

Using white yarn,

R1: Ch 2, 5 sc in second ch from hook.

R2: Sc 2 in each sc around. (10 sts)

R3: *Sc 1, 2 sc in next sc*, rep 5 times. (15 sts)

R4: Sc 15.

Sl st 1 and fasten off, leaving long tail for sewing. Embroider nose, mouth, and whiskers; set aside.

Head

Using tan yarn,

R1: Ch 2, 5 sc in second ch from hook.

R2: Sc 2 in each sc around. (10 sts)

R3: *Sc 1, 2 sc in next sc*, rep 5 times. (15 sts)

R4: *Sc 2, 2 sc in next sc*, rep 5 times. (20 sts)

R5: *Sc 3, 2 sc in next sc*, rep 5 times. (25 sts)

R6: *Sc 4, 2 sc in next sc*, rep 5 times. (30 sts)

R7–13: Sc 30.

R14: *Sc 4, dec 1*, rep 5 times. (25 sts)

R15: *Sc 3, dec 1*, rep 5 times. (20 sts)

Work on face: Sew muzzle in place; position and attach eyes.

R16: *Sc 2, dec 1, rep 5 times. (15 sts)

R17: *Sc 1, dec 1, rep 5 times. (10 sts)

Stuff firmly.

R18: Dec 5 times. (5 sts)

Fasten off.

Ears (Make 2.)

Using tan yarn,

R1: Ch 2, 5 sc in second ch from hook.

R2: Sc 5.

R3: Sc 2 in each sc around. (10 sts)

Sl st 1 and fasten off, leaving long tail for sewing. Sew open end tog and sew to head.

Body

Using tan yarn,

R1: Ch 2, 5 sc in second ch from hook.

R2: Sc 2 in each sc around. (10 sts)

R3: *Sc 1, 2 sc in next sc*, rep 5 times. (15 sts)

R4–9: Sc 15.

Sl st 1 and fasten off, leaving long tail for sewing. Stuff and sew to head.

Legs (Make 4.)

Use tan yarn for one leg and white for the others.

R1: Ch 2, sc 5 in second ch from hook.

R2–5: Sc 5.

Sl st 1 and fasten off, leaving long tail for sewing. Sew open end tog and sew to body.

Tail

Using tan yarn,

R1: Ch 2, sc 5 in second ch from hook.

R2 and 3: Sc 5.

Change to white yarn,

R4–11: Sc 5.

Sl st 1 and fasten off, leaving long tail for sewing. Sew to body.

BED

Using G hook and yellow yarn,

R1: Ch 2, 6 sc in second ch from hook.

R2: Sc 2 in each sc around. (12 sts)

R3: *Sc 1, 2 sc in next sc*, rep 6 times. (18 sts)

R4: *Sc 2, 2 sc in next sc*, rep 6 times. (24 sts)

R5: *Sc 3, 2 sc in next sc*, rep 6 times. (30 sts)

R6: *Sc 4, 2 sc in next sc*, rep 6 times. (36 sts)

R7: *Sc 5, 2 sc in next sc*, rep 6 times. (42 sts)

R8: *Sc 6, 2 sc in next sc*, rep 6 times. (48 sts)

R9: *Sc 7, 2 sc in next sc*, rep 6 times. (54 sts)

R10: *Sc 8, 2 sc in next sc*, rep 6 times. (60 sts)

R11–20: Sc 60.

Sl st 1 and fasten off, leaving long tail for sewing. With RS facing you, fold edge over all around and sew edge to WS along row 12 of bed, stuffing lightly as you go.

FINISHING

Make a little ball of yarn for your kitty to play with while she's tucked in her bed.

PRINCESS FROG
AND WATER LILY THRONE

As much as Oli likes pigs, Martina loves frogs, which kind of surprised me at first because frogs don't seem too cute and cuddly to me. The first time her frog love became evident was in the Central Park Zoo's store. They had the cutest stuffed bunnies and dolphins and bears, which I kept showing two-year-old Marti, but none of them would do. She was set on a little green frog that she still carries around. She also loves pretending to be a princess, with lots of jewelry and dresses, so a princess frog with a really cute—and pink!—throne seemed more than appropriate for her.

FINISHED SIZES

Princess frog: Approx 4" tall

Water lily throne: Approx 2½" tall

MATERIALS

Worsted-weight yarn in green, yellow, and pink

Size G/6 (4 mm) crochet hook

9 mm plastic eyes with safety backings

Black embroidery floss and embroidery needle

Tapestry needle

Fiberfill or stuffing of your choice

PRINCESS FROG

Using green yarn,

Eyes (Make 2.)

R1: Ch 2, 6 sc in second ch from hook.

R2: Sc 2 in each sc around. (12 sts)

R3–5: Sc 12.

Sl st 1 and fasten off, leaving long tail for sewing. Position and attach eyes, stuff, and set aside.

Head

R1: Ch 2, 6 sc in second ch from hook.

R2: Sc 2 in each sc around. (12 sts)

R3: *Sc 1, 2 sc in next sc*, rep 6 times. (18 sts)

R4: *Sc 2, 2 sc in next sc*, rep 6 times. (24 sts)

R5: *Sc 3, 2 sc in next sc*, rep 6 times. (30 sts)

R6: *Sc 4, 2 sc in next sc*, rep 6 times. (36 sts)

R7–12: Sc 36.

Work on face: Sew eyes in place; embroider mouth.

R13: *Sc 4, dec 1*, rep 6 times. (30 sts)

R14: *Sc 3, dec 1*, rep 6 times. (24 sts)

R15: *Sc 2, dec 1*, rep 6 times. (18 sts)

R16: *Sc 1, dec 1*, rep 6 times. (12 sts)

Stuff head.

R17: Dec 6 times. (6 sts)

Fasten off.

Body

R1: Ch 2, 6 sc in second ch from hook.

R2: Sc 2 in each sc around. (12 sts)

R3: *Sc 1, 2 sc in next sc*, rep 6 times. (18 sts)

R4: *Sc 2, 2 sc in next sc*, rep 6 times. (24 sts)

R5–10: Sc 24.

Sl st 1 and fasten off, leaving long tail for sewing. Stuff and sew to head.

Arms and Legs (Make 4.)

R1: Ch 2, 6 sc in second ch from hook.

R2–6: Sc 6.

Sl st 1 and fasten off, leaving long tail for sewing. Sew open end tog and sew to body.

WATER LILY THRONE

Cushion

Using yellow yarn,

R1: Ch 2, 5 sc in second ch from hook.

R2: Sc 2 in each sc around. (10 sts)

R3: *Sc 1, 2 sc in next sc*, rep 5 times. (15 sts)

R4: *Sc 2, 2 sc in next sc*, rep 5 times. (20 sts)

R5: *Sc 3, 2 sc in next sc*, rep 5 times. (25 sts)

R6: *Sc 4, 2 sc in next sc*, rep 5 times. (30 sts)

R7: *Sc 5, 2 sc in next sc*, rep 5 times. (35 sts)

R8: Sc 35.

R9: Sc 35 through back loops only.

R10: Sc 35.

R11: Sc 35 through back loops only.

R12: Sc 35.

R13: *Sc 5, dec 1*, rep 5 times. (30 sts)

R14: *Sc 4, dec 1*, rep 5 times. (25 sts)

R15: *Sc 3, dec 1*, rep 5 times. (20 sts)

R16: *Sc 2, dec 1*, rep 5 times. (15 sts)

Stuff lightly.

R17: *Sc 1, dec 1*, rep 5 times. (10 sts)

R18: Dec 5 times. (5 sts)

Fasten off.

Petals (Make 4 Short and 7 Long.)

Using pink yarn,

R1: Ch 2, 5 sc in second ch from hook.

R2: Sc 5.

R3: Sc 2 in each sc around. (10 sts)

R4–8: Sc 10.

For short petals: Fasten off, leaving long tail for sewing. Sew open end tog and sew them next to each other on R9 (where you worked into the back loops) of cushion.

For long petals:

R9 and 10: Sc 10.

Sl st 1 and fasten off, leaving long tail for sewing. Sew open end tog and sew long petals next to each other behind short petals on R10 of cushion.

CROWN

Using yellow yarn,

Loosely ch 10, close with sl st to form a ring.

R1: Sc 10 inside ring.

R2: *Sl st 1, dc 1*, rep all around.

Sl st 1 and fasten off, leaving long tail for sewing. Sew to frog's head.

HAPPY LITTLE SWEET SNACKS: FLAN, HOT COCOA, AND CAKE

Snack time is my favorite time of the day. What better way to remind me of that than crocheting happy little snacks! Just like the ones in my first book, *Amigurumi World*, these are super fast to whip up, and make the cutest little gifts—and the sweetest pincushions.

FINISHED SIZES

Little flan: Approx 2½" tall
Hot cocoa: Approx 2" tall
Little cake: Approx 3" tall

MATERIALS

Worsted-weight yarn in yellow, brown, red, green, tan, white, pink, and blue
Size F/5 (3.75 mm) crochet hook
9 mm plastic eyes with safety backings
Small piece of pink craft felt
Sewing thread and sharp needle
Black embroidery floss and embroidery needle
Tapestry needle
Fiberfill or stuffing of your choice

FLAN

Flan

Using brown yarn,
R1: Ch 2, 6 sc in second ch from hook.
R2: Sc 2 in each sc around. (12 sts)
R3: *Sc 1, 2 sc in next sc*, rep 6 times. (18 sts)
R4: *Sc 2, 2 sc in next sc*, rep 6 times. (24 sts)
R5: *Sc 3, 2 sc in next sc*, rep 6 times. (30 sts)

R6: *Sc 4, 2 sc in next sc*, rep 6 times. (36 sts)

Change to yellow yarn,

R7: Through back loops only, *sc 4, dec 1*, rep 6 times. (30 sts)

R8: *Sc 4, 2 sc in next sc*, rep 6 times. (36 sts)

R9–14: Sc 36.

Work on face: Position and attach eyes; embroider mouth.

R15: Sc 36 through back loops only.

R16: *Sc 4, dec 1*, rep 6 times. (30 sts)

R17: *Sc 3, dec 1*, rep 6 times. (24 sts)

R18: *Sc 2, dec 1*, rep 6 times. (18 sts)

R19: *Sc 1, dec 1*, rep 6 times. (12 sts)

Stuff.

R20: Dec 6 times. (6 sts)

Fasten off.

Cherry

Using red yarn,

R1: Ch 2, 6 sc in second ch from hook.

R2: Sc 2 in each sc around. (12 sts)

R3–6: Sc 12.

Stuff.

R7: Dec 6 times. (6 sts)

Fasten off, leaving long tail for sewing.

Leaf

Using green yarn,

Loosely ch 6. Starting in second ch from hook, sl st 1, dc 1, tr 2, sl st 1.

Fasten off, leaving long tail for sewing. Sew leaf to bottom of cherry and sew cherry to top of flan.

HOT COCOA

Cup

Using blue yarn,

R1: Ch 2, 6 sc in second ch from hook.

R2: Sc 2 in each sc around. (12 sts)

R3: *Sc 1, 2 sc in next sc*, rep 6 times. (18 sts)

R4: *Sc 2, 2 sc in next sc*, rep 6 times. (24 sts)

R5: *Sc 3, 2 sc in next sc*, rep 6 times. (30 sts)

R6–13: Sc 36.

Sl st 1 and fasten off.

Work on face: Position and attach eyes; embroider mouth. For cheeks, use the pattern to cut 2 circles from pink felt and sew to face.

Handle

Using blue yarn,

R1: Ch 2, 4 sc in second ch from hook.

R2–9: Sc 4.

Sl st 1 and fasten off, leaving long tail for sewing. Sew to cup (there's no need to stuff handle).

Hot Cocoa

Using brown yarn,

R1: Ch 2, 6 sc in second ch from hook.

R2: Sc 2 in each sc around. (12 sts)

R3: *Sc 1, 2 sc in next sc*, rep 6 times. (18 sts)

R4: *Sc 2, 2 sc in next sc*, rep 6 times. (24 sts)

R5: *Sc 3, 2 sc in next sc*, rep 6 times. (30 sts)

Sl st 1 and fasten off, leaving long tail for sewing. Stuff cup and sew hot cocoa circle inside cup, 1 row below top edge.

Marshmallow

Using white yarn,

R1: Ch 2, 5 sc in second ch from hook.

R2: Sc 2 in each sc around. (10 sts)

R3: Sc 10.

Sl st 1 and fasten off, leaving long tail for sewing. Stuff and sew to hot cocoa.

Hot cocoa cheek

Cake

Start crocheting cake at the top using white yarn.

R1: Ch 2, 6 sc in second ch from hook.

R2: Sc 2 in each sc around. (12 sts)

R3: *Sc 1, 2 sc in next sc*, rep 6 times. (18 sts)

R4: *Sc 2, 2 sc in next sc*, rep 6 times. (24 sts)

Change to tan yarn,

R5: Sc 24 through back loops only.

R6–8: Sc 24.

Change to white yarn,

R9: Through front loops only, *sc 3, 2 sc in next sc*, rep 6 times. (30 sts)

R10: *Sc 4, 2 sc in next sc*, rep 6 times. (36 sts)

R11: *Sc 5, 2 sc in next sc*, rep 6 times. (42 sts)

Change to tan yarn,

R12: Sc 42 through back loops only.

R13–17: Sc 36.

Work on face: Position and attach eyes; embroider mouth.

R18: Through back loops only, *sc 5, dec 1*, rep 6 times. (36 sts)

R19: *Sc 4, dec 1*, rep 6 times. (20 sts)

R20: *Sc 3, dec 1*, rep 6 times. (24 sts)

R21: *Sc 2, dec 1*, rep 6 times. (18 sts)

Stuff.

R22: *Sc 1, dec 1*, rep 6 times. (12 sts)

R23: Dec 6 times. (6 sts)

Fasten off.

Cherry and leaf: Work as for cherry and leaf in flan (see page 57), except use pink yarn for cherry.

LITTLE TUGBOAT

I used to have a little plastic tugboat when I was a young girl. It was great to play with in the water but had no hugging potential. This crocheted one can't go in the water, but it's soft and plush . . . and huggable!

FINISHED SIZE

Approx 4½" high x 6" long

MATERIALS

Worsted-weight yarn in brown, red, yellow, blue, and white

Size G/6 (4 mm) crochet hook

12 mm plastic eyes with safety backings

Black embroidery floss and embroidery needle

Tapestry needle

Fiberfill or stuffing of your choice

HULL

Start crocheting hull at bottom using red yarn.

Ch 11.

R1: Sc 10 starting at second bump at back of ch (see page 76), ch 3, sc 10 on opposite side of ch (both loops of ch). (20 sc and 3 ch)

R2: Ch 3, *sc 10, sc 4 in ch-3 sp*, rep once on other side. (28 sts)

R3: *Sc 10, sc 2 in each of next 4 sts*, rep once on other side. (36 sts)

R4: *Sc 11, sc 2 in each of next 6 sts, sc 1*, rep once on other side. (48 sts)

R5: *Sc 13, sc 2 in next st, sc 6, sc 2 in next st, sc 3*, rep once on other side. (52 sts)

R6: *Sc 16, sc 2 in each of next 4 sts, sc 6*, rep once on other side. (60 sts)

R7: *Sc 19, sc 2 in each of next 2 sts, sc 9*, rep once on other side. (64 sts)

R8: *Sc 20, sc 2 in next 2 sts, sc 10*, rep once on other side. (68 sts)

R9: Sc 68 through back loops only.

R10–17: Sc 68.

Sl st 1 and fasten off.

DECK

Using brown yarn,

Rep instructions for hull through R8.

R9: Sc 68.

Sl st 1 and fasten off, leaving long tail for sewing. Position deck inside hull (approx ½" below edge of hull) sew ¾ of the way around, stuff, and finish sewing.

HEAD

Using blue yarn,

R1: Ch 2, 5 sc in second ch from hook.

R2: Sc 2 in each sc around. (10 sts)

R3: *Sc 1, 2 sc in next sc*, rep 5 times. (15 sts)

R4: *Sc 2, 2 sc in next sc*, rep 5 times. (20 sts)

R5: *Sc 3, 2 sc in next sc*, rep 5 times. (25 sts)

R6: *Sc 4, 2 sc in next sc*, rep 5 times. (30 sts)

R7: *Sc 5, 2 sc in next sc*, rep 5 times. (35 sts)

R8: *Sc 6, 2 sc in next sc*, rep 5 times. (40 sts)

R9: Through back loops only, *sc 6, dec 1*, rep 5 times. (35 sts)

R10–15: Sc 35.

Sl st 1 and fasten off, leaving long tail for sewing.

Work on face: Position and attach eyes; embroider mouth. Stuff and sew to deck.

HAT

Using white yarn,

R1: Ch 2, 5 sc in second ch from hook.

R2: Sc 2 in each sc around. (10 sts)

R3: *Sc 1, 2 sc in next sc*, rep 5 times. (15 sts)

R4: *Sc 2, 2 sc in next sc*, rep 5 times. (20 sts)

R5–7: Sc 20.

R8: Sc 20, turn.

R9: Through back loops only, *sc 3, 2 sc in next sc*, rep 5 times. Do not turn. (25 sts)

R10–12: Working in rnd again, sc 25.

Sl st 1 and fasten off. Stuff lightly and sew to head using white yarn.

BUMPERS (Make 4.)

Using yellow yarn,

Ch 15.

R1: Join first and last sts with sl st to form ring (being careful not to twist sts) and sc 15 inside the ring.

R2–6: Sc 15.

Sl st 1 and fasten off, leaving long tail for sewing. Fold piece and sew edges tog to form donut shape. Fasten off, leaving long tail for sewing. Sew 2 bumpers to each side of boat.

LiTTLE BaBieS:
TiGER, LiON, BEaR, anD ELePHanT

These four little babies share the same body, head, and extremities. All you need to do is add the appropriate ears, trunk, tail, or mane for the animal. Soon you'll be a pro and I know you can figure out how to alter the details to create many more little babies!

FiNiSHED SiZE

Each animal: Approx 3" tall

MaTERiaLS

Worsted-weight yarn in orange, gold, tan, blue, gray, and white

Size F/5 (3.75 mm) crochet hook

9 mm plastic eyes with safety backings

Small piece of black craft felt

Black embroidery floss and embroidery needle

Tapestry needle

Fiberfill or stuffing of your choice

Glue (optional)

LiTTLE BaBieS

Muzzle for Lion, Tiger, and Bear

Using yarn color of your choice,

R1: Ch 2, 5 sc in second ch from hook.

R2: Sc 2 in each sc around. (10 sts)

R3: *Sc 1, 2 sc in next sc*, rep 5 times. (15 sts)

R4: Sc 15.

Sl st 1 and fasten off, leaving long tail for sewing. Embroider nose and mouth; set aside.

Eye Roundies for Elephant (Make 2.)

Using white yarn,

R1: Ch 2, 6 sc in second ch from hook.

R2: Sc 2 in each sc around. (12 sts)

Sl st 1 and fasten off, leaving long tail for sewing. Put 9 mm plastic eyes through middle hole and set aside.

Elephant Trunk

Using gray yarn,

R1: Ch 2, 5 sc in second ch from hook.

R2: Sc 2 in each sc around. (10 sts)

R3–6: Sc 10.

Work on face: Position and attach eyes. For lion, tiger, and bear: sew muzzle in place. For elephant: sew trunk so it curves up, add eye roundies and sew them in place, and embroider mouth.

R15: *Sc 2, dec 1*, rep 6 times. (18 sts)

Stuff head.

R16: *Sc 1, dec 1*, rep 6 times. (12 sts)

R17: Dec 6 times. (6 sts)

Fasten off.

Body

R1: Ch 2, 6 sc in second ch from hook.

R2: Sc 2 in each sc around. (12 sts)

R3: *Sc 1, 2 sc in next sc*, rep 6 times. (18 sts)

R4–8: Sc 18.

Sl st 1 and fasten off, leaving long tail for sewing. Stuff and sew to head.

Arms and Legs (Make 4 for Each Animal.)

R1: Ch 2, 4 sc in second ch from hook.

R2: Sc 2 in each sc around. (8 sts)

R3–7: Sc 8.

Sl st 1 and fasten off, leaving long tail for sewing. Stuff, sew open end tog, and sew to body.

Lion and Tiger Ears (Make 2 for Each Animal.)

R1: Ch 2, 5 sc in second ch from hook.

R2: Sc 5.

R3: Sc 2 in each sc around. (10 sts)

Sl st 1 and fasten off, leaving long tail for sewing. Sew open end tog and sew to head.

R7: Sc 5 through front loops only, dc 5.

R8: Sc 5, sl st 1, leaving 5 dc unworked.

Fasten off, leaving long tail for sewing. Stuff and set aside.

The head, body, and extremities are the same for all four babies.

Head

R1: Ch 2, sc 6 in second ch from hook.

R2: Sc 2 in each sc around. (12 sts)

R3: *Sc 1, 2 sc in next sc*, rep 6 times. (18 sts)

R4: *Sc 2, 2 sc in next sc*, rep 6 times. (24 sts)

R5: *Sc 3, 2 sc in next sc*, rep 6 times. (30 sts)

R6–13: Sc 30.

R14: *Sc 3, dec 1*, rep 6 times. (24 sts)

Lion Mane

Using tan yarn,

Loosely ch 33. Sl st 1 in second ch from hook, *ch 6, sl st in next ch*, rep to end.

Fasten off, leaving long tail for sewing. Sew both ends tog and place mane on lion's head behind ears as if it were a headband; sew in place.

Lion and Tiger Tail (Make 1 for Each Animal.)

Loosely ch 16. Starting in second ch from hook, sl st 15. Fasten off, leaving long tail for sewing. Sew to body.

Elephant Ears (Make 2.)

Using gray yarn,

R1: Ch 2, 6 sc in second ch from hook.

R2: Sc 2 in each sc around. (12 sts)

R3: *Sc 1, 2 sc in next sc*, rep 6 times. (18 sts)

R4 and 5: Sc 18.

R6: *Sc 1, dec 1*, rep 6 times. (12 sts)

R7: Dec 6 times. (6 sts)

Sl st 1 and fasten off, leaving long tail for sewing. Sew open end tog and sew to head.

Bear Ears (Make 2.)

Using white yarn,

R1: Ch 2, 5 sc in second ch from hook.

R2: Sc 2 in each sc around. (10 sts)

R3: Sc 10.

Sl st 1 and fasten off, leaving long tail for sewing. Sew open end tog and sew to head.

Tiger Stripes

Use the patterns to cut 4 rectangles from black felt; sew or glue to face.

Top stripe. Cut 1.

Top stripe. Cut 1.

Side stripe. Cut 2.

Tiger stripes

MOM AND BABY FOX

Oli's in second grade already (I can't believe it!), and she reads a lot. Every couple of days she finishes a big chapter book and is always asking for more. The last one we bought for her was *Fantastic Mr. Fox* by Roald Dahl, and I thought it'd be nice to have some amigurumi foxes to go with it.

FINISHED SIZES

Mom fox: Approx 5½" tall
Baby fox: Approx 4" tall

MATERIALS

Worsted-weight yarn in orange, white, and blue

Size G/6 (4 mm) crochet hook

9 and 12 mm plastic eyes with safety backings

Black embroidery floss and embroidery needle

Tapestry needle

Fiberfill or stuffing of your choice

MOM FOX

Muzzle

Using orange yarn,

R1: Ch 2, 6 sc in second ch from hook.

R2: 2 sc in each sc around. (12 sts)

R3 and 4: Sc 12.

R5: *Sc 1, 2 sc in next sc*, rep 6 times. (18 sts)

R6: Sc 18.

Sl st 1 and fasten off, leaving long tail for sewing. Embroider nose and mouth and set aside.

Eye Roundies (Make 2.)

Using white yarn,

R1: Ch 2, 6 sc in second ch from hook.

R2: 2 sc in each sc around. (12 sts)

R3: *Sc 1, 2 sc in next sc*, rep 6 times. (18 sts)

Sl st 1 and fasten off, leaving long tail for sewing. Put 12 mm eye through middle hole and set aside.

Head

Using orange yarn,

R1: Ch 2, 6 sc in second ch from hook.

R2: 2 sc in each sc around. (12 sts)

R3: *Sc 1, 2 sc in next sc*, rep 6 times. (18 sts)

R4: *Sc 2, 2 sc in next sc*, rep 6 times. (24 sts)

R5: *Sc 3, 2 sc in next sc*, rep 6 times. (30 sts)

R6: *Sc 4, 2 sc in next sc*, rep 6 times. (36 sts)

R7: *Sc 5, 2 sc in next sc*, rep 6 times. (42 sts)

R8–17: Sc 42.

R18: *Sc 5, dec 1*, rep 6 times. (36 sts)

R19: *Sc 4, dec 1*, rep 6 times. (30 sts)

Work on face: Stuff muzzle a little and sew to face. Position and attach eyes (with eye roundies); sew eye roundies in place.

R20: *Sc 3, dec 1*, rep 6 times. (24 sts)

R21: *Sc 2, dec 1*, rep 6 times. (18 sts)

Stuff head.

R22: *Sc 1, dec 1*, rep 6 times. (12 sts)

R23: Dec 6 times. (6 sts)

Fasten off.

Ears (Make 2.)

Using orange yarn,

R1: Ch 2, 5 sc in second ch from hook.

R2: Sc 5.

R3: 2 sc in each sc around. (10 sts)

R4 and 5: Sc 10.

R6: *Sc 1, 2 sc in next sc*, rep 5 times. (15 sts)

R7: Sc 15.

Sl st 1 and fasten off, leaving long tail for sewing. Sew open end tog and sew to head.

Body

Using orange yarn,

R1: Ch 2, 6 sc in second ch from hook.

R2: 2 sc in each sc around. (12 sts)

R3: *Sc 1, 2 sc in next sc*, rep 6 times. (18 sts)

R4: *Sc 2, 2 sc in next sc*, rep 6 times. (24 sts)

R5: *Sc 3, 2 sc in next sc*, rep 6 times. (30 sts)

R6–13: Sc 30.

Sl st 1 and fasten off, leaving long tail for sewing. Stuff and sew to head.

Arms and Legs (Make 4.)

Using orange yarn,

R1: Ch 2, 5 sc in second ch from hook.

R2: 2 sc in each sc around. (10 sts)

R3–8: Sc 10.

Sl st 1 and fasten off, leaving long tail for sewing. Stuff, sew open end of arms tog, and then sew all to body.

Tail

Using white yarn,

R1: Ch 2, 6 sc in second ch from hook.

R2: Sc 6.

R3: *Sc 1, 2 sc in next sc*, rep 3 times. (9 sts)

R4: Sc 9.

R5: *Sc 2, 2 sc in next sc*, rep 3 times. (12 sts)

R6: Sc 12.

Change to orange yarn,

R7: *Sc 3, 2 sc in next sc*, rep 3 times. (15 sts)

R8–14: Sc 15.

Stuff almost to top.

R15: *Sc 3, dec 1*, rep 3 times. (12 sts)

R16: *Sc 2, dec 1*, rep 3 times. (9 sts)

R17: *Sc 1, dec 1*, rep 3 times. (6 sts)

Sl st 1 and fasten off, leaving long tail for sewing. Sew to body.

Little Scarf

Using blue yarn, loosely ch 72 and fasten off. Wrap around Mom's neck.

BaBY FOX

Muzzle

Using orange yarn,

R1: Ch 2, 6 sc in second ch from hook.

R2: Sc 6.

R3–5: 2 sc in each sc around. (12 sts)

Sl st 1 and fasten off, leaving long tail for sewing. Embroider nose and smile and set aside.

Eye Roundies (Make 2.)

Using white yarn,

R1: Ch 2, 6 sc in second ch from hook.

R2: 2 sc in each sc around. (12 sts)

Sl st 1 and fasten off, leaving long tail for sewing. Put 9 mm eye through middle hole and set aside.

Head

Using orange yarn,

R1: Ch 2, 6 sc in second ch from hook.

R2: 2 sc in each sc around. (12 sts)

R3: *Sc 1, 2 sc in next sc*, rep 6 times. (18 sts)

R4: *Sc 2, 2 sc in next sc*, rep 6 times. (24 sts)

R5: *Sc 3, 2 sc in next sc*, rep 6 times. (30 sts)

R6–13: Sc 30.

Work on face: Stuff muzzle a little and sew to face. Position and attach eyes (with eye roundies); sew eye roundies in place.

R14: *Sc 3, dec 1*, rep 6 times. (24 sts)

R15: *Sc 2, dec 1*, rep 6 times. (18 sts)

R16: *Sc 1, dec 1*, rep 6 times. (12 sts)

Stuff head.

R17: Dec 6 times. (6 sts)

Fasten off.

Ears (Make 2.)

Using orange yarn,

R1: Ch 2, 5 sc in second ch from hook.

R2: Sc 5.

R3: 2 sc in each sc around. (10 sts)

R4–6: Sc 10.

Sl st 1 and fasten off, leaving long tail for sewing. Sew open end tog and sew to head.

Body

Using orange yarn,

R1: Ch 2, 6 sc in second ch from hook.

R2: 2 sc in each sc around. (12 sts)

R3: *Sc 1, 2 sc in next sc*, rep 6 times. (18 sts)

R4 and 5: Sc 18.

Change to blue yarn,

R6–8: Sc 18.

Sl st 1 and fasten off, leaving long tail for sewing. Stuff and sew to head.

Arms and Legs (Make 4.)

Using orange yarn,

R1: Ch 2, 5 sc in second ch from hook.

R2–4: Sc 5.

Sl st 1 and fasten off, leaving long tail for sewing. Sew open end of arms tog, and then sew all to body.

Tail

Using white yarn,

R1: Ch 2, 6 sc in second ch from hook.

R2: Sc 6.

R3: *Sc 1, 2 sc in next sc*, rep 3 times. (9 sts)

Change to orange yarn,

R4: Sc 9.

R5: *Sc 2, 2 sc in next sc*, rep 3 times. (12 sts)

R6–8: Sc 12.

Stuff almost to top.

R9: Dec 6 times. (6 sts)

Sl st 1 and fasten off, leaving long tail to close 6-st hole. Sew to body.

SHY LiTTLe UNiCORN

I've been meaning to make a unicorn for the longest time, but I was never successful. I showed my first attempt to Oli and she said it was a cow! (She couldn't explain the horn.) Marti said my second attempt was a pig! So when I finished this one and they both said it was "a cute little unicorn," I knew I had finally finally succeeded. You can also make it brown and without the horn and have a pony, or maybe even add spots to make Oli's cow.

FiNiSHeD SiZe

Approx 4½" tall x 6" long

MATeRiaLS

Worsted-weight yarn in white and pink

Scraps of worsted-weight yarn in yellow, red, orange, green, purple, and blue

Size G/6 (4 mm) crochet hook

9 mm plastic eyes with safety backings

Small piece of pink craft felt

Tapestry needle

Fiberfill or stuffing of your choice

HeaD

Using pink yarn,

R1: Ch 2, 7 sc in second ch from hook.

R2: 2 sc in each sc around. (14 sts)

R3: *Sc 1, 2 sc in next sc*, rep 7 times. (21 sts)

R4: *Sc 2, 2 sc in next sc*, rep 7 times. (28 sts)

R5: *Sc 3, 2 sc in next sc*, rep 7 times. (35 sts)

R6–9: Sc 35.

Change to white yarn,

R10: Sc 35.

R11: *Sc 3, dec 1*, rep 7 times. (28 sts)

R12 and 13: Sc 28.

Work on muzzle: For nostrils, use the pattern on page 72 to cut 2 circles from pink felt and sew them to unicorn's nose.

R14–21: Sc 28.

R22: *Sc 2, dec 1*, rep 7 times. (21 sts)

Position and attach plastic eyes.

R23: *Sc 1, dec 1*, rep 7 times. (14 sts)

Stuff firmly.

R24: Dec 7 times. (7 sts)

Fasten off, leaving long tail to close 7-st hole.

Ears (Make 2.)

Using white yarn,

R1: Ch 2, 4 sc in second ch from hook.

R2: 2 sc in each sc around. (8 sts)

R3–7: Sc 8.

Sl st 1 and fasten off, leaving long tail for sewing. Sew to head.

Horn

Using yellow yarn,

R1: Ch 2, 4 sc in second ch from hook.

R2: Sc 4.

R3: *Sc 1, 2 sc in next sc*, rep one more time. (6 sts)

R4–8: Sc 6.

Sl st 1 and fasten off, leaving long tail for sewing. Sew to head.

Body

Using white yarn,

R1: Ch 2, 6 sc in second ch from hook.

R2: 2 sc in each sc around. (12 sts)

R3: *Sc 1, 2 sc in next sc*, rep 6 times. (18 sts)

R4: *Sc 2, 2 sc in next sc*, rep 6 times. (24 sts)

R5–10: Sc 24.

R11: *Sc 2, dec 1*, rep 6 times. (18 sts)

R12–14: Sc 18.

R15: *Sc 1, dec 1*, rep 6 times. (12 sts)

R16 and 17: Sc 12.

Sl st 1 and fasten off, leaving long tail for sewing. Stuff and sew to head.

Legs (Make 4.)

Using pink yarn,

R1: Ch 2, 6 sc in second ch from hook.

R2: 2 sc in each sc around. (12 sts)

R3: Sc 12.

Change to white yarn,

R4–14: Sc 12.

Stuff lightly.

R15: Dec 6 times. (6 sts)

Fasten off, leaving long tail for sewing. Stuff a little, sew open end tog, and sew to body.

Mane

This takes a while, but it makes the unicorn look so cute.

Make 6 with red, 6 with orange, 6 with green, 6 with purple, and 6 with blue yarn.

Ch 12 and fasten off, leaving long tail for sewing. Sew to head, creating a part down the middle of the mane.

Tail (Make 4.)

Ch 24 and fasten off, leaving long tail for sewing. Sew to body.

Unicorn nostril

General Guidelines

Simple crochet skills are all you need to make these delightful amigurumi.

Yarn

The toys in this book are crocheted using worsted-weight yarn and a size G/6 (4 mm) crochet hook, and occasionally a size F/5 (3.75 mm) or E/4 (3.5 mm) hook. A list of the yarn brands I used for the samples in this book can be found on page 78, but it doesn't really matter which brand you use.

Making amigurumi is a great way to use up leftover yarn. Choose colors similar to mine, or be creative and come up with your own color combinations! People often ask how many toys you can make from one 100-gram skein of worsted-weight yarn. While it varies, depending on the pattern and how tightly you crochet, I can usually get two to three of the larger animals and many, many small toys from just one 100-gram skein of main color. Of course you'll need other colors for some body parts and embellishments.

Gauge, Tension, and Hook Sizes

The measurements given for each toy are approximate and based on the way I crochet. I crochet pretty tightly, and my gauge is as follows:

4 sts and 5 rows = 1" with G hook and worsted-weight yarn

5 sts and 6 rows = 1" with F hook and worsted-weight yarn

The finished toy size, however, isn't really that important, so don't worry if your gauge is different from mine. Depending on your tension and the yarn you use, your toys might end up being a little bit smaller or larger than the ones I made. Changing to a bigger or smaller hook will give you a bigger or smaller toy, respectively.

Stitches

Simple stitches are used for these amigurumi projects, making them perfect for beginners.

Chain (ch). Make a slipknot and place it on the hook. Yarn over the hook, draw the yarn through the slipknot, and let the slipknot slide off the hook. *Yarn over the hook, draw the yarn through the new loop, and let the loop slide off the hook. Repeat from * for the desired number of chains.

Slip stitch (sl st). A slip stitch is used to move across one or more stitches. Insert the hook into the stitch, yarn over the hook, and pull through both stitches at once.

Single crochet (sc). *Insert the hook into the chain or stitch indicated, yarn over the hook, and pull through the chain or stitch (two loops remain on hook).

Yarn over the hook and pull through the remaining two loops on the hook. Repeat from * for the required number of stitches.

Back-post single crochet (BPsc). Insert the hook from the back around the vertical section, or post, of the single crochet stitch in the previous row and complete the single crochet stitch as usual. Repeat as directed to get a nice, slightly raised, braid-like row of stitches.

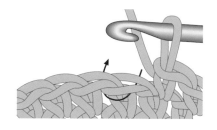

Single crochet increase. Work two single crochet stitches into the same stitch.

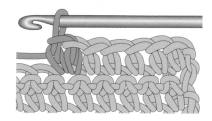

Single crochet decrease (dec). (Insert the hook into the next stitch, yarn over, pull up a loop) twice; yarn over and pull through all three loops on the hook.

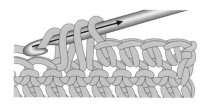

Half double crochet (hdc). *Yarn over the hook and insert the hook into the chain or stitch indicated. Yarn over the hook and pull through the stitch (three loops remain on the hook).

Yarn over the hook and pull through all three loops on the hook. Repeat from * for the required number of stitches.

Double crochet (dc). *Yarn over the hook and insert the hook into the chain or stitch indicated. Yarn over the hook and pull through the stitch (three loops are on the hook); yarn over the hook and pull through two loops on the hook (two loops remain on the hook).

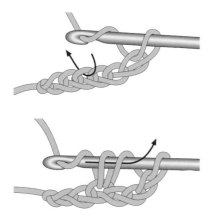

Yarn over the hook and pull through the remaining two loops on the hook (one loop remains on the hook). Repeat from * for the required number of stitches.

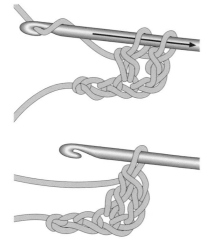

Triple crochet (tr). *Yarn over the hook twice, insert the hook into the chain or stitch indicated. *Yarn over the hook and pull through the stitch (four loops on the hook); yarn over the hook and pull through two loops on the hook (three loops remain on the hook).

(Yarn over the hook and pull through two loops on the hook) twice (one loop remains on the hook). Repeat from * for the required number of stitches.

WORKING IN CHAIN LOOPS

When crocheting the first row into the beginning chain, the first row of stitches is generally worked into one or both loops on the right side of the chain.

Crocheting into top loop

Crocheting into both loops

For some projects, the first row of stitches is worked in the "bump" on the wrong side of the chain.

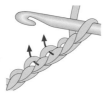

WORKING IN STITCH LOOPS

The majority of the stitches are worked in both loops of the stitches from the previous row. There are a few projects where you will work a row into the back loop or the front loop of the stitch.

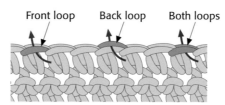

Front loop   Back loop   Both loops

CROCHETING IN THE ROUND

When crocheting in the round, I crochet around and around, forming a continuous spiral. To keep track of where the rounds begin and end, you can mark the end or beginning of a round with a safety pin, stitch marker, or little piece of yarn pulled through one of the stitches. At the end of the last round, slip-stitch in the first single crochet of the previous round and fasten the yarn off.

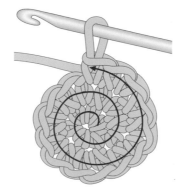

HOW TO CHANGE YARN COLORS

Some projects require alternating two colors in the body. To do this, work the last stitch of a round until one step remains in the stitch; then work the last step with the new color and continue the round in the new color. Continue to the end of the round and change color in the same manner.

ADDING FACES

Although I've used plastic eyes with safety backings on all of the toys, you can instead embroider the eyes, use buttons, or cut out and sew on little pieces of felt. For each pattern, eye sizes are given in millimeters.

SAFETY

Plastic eyes with safety backings are nearly impossible to take out—I've tried! I would not, however, give a toy with plastic eyes (or buttons) to children younger than three years old unless they are being supervised at all times while playing with them. Eyes cut from craft felt or embroidered eyes are a better choice for young children.

The templates for the muzzles and any other pieces to be cut from felt are included with each project. Cut the felt pieces with sharp scissors to get nice, smooth edges. Using embroidery floss and a needle, I use simple stitches to "draw" the faces on the felt before attaching the felt pieces to the face. Sew pieces of felt on with a sharp needle and matching sewing thread. Use a very small running stitch close to the edge of the piece.

Mouths. For a simple mouth, bring the needle out at point A and insert the needle at point B, leaving a loose strand of yarn to form the mouth. Once you're happy with the shape of the mouth, bring the needle out again at point C, cross over the loose strand of yarn, and insert the needle at point D to make a tiny stitch. Secure the ends on the wrong side.

Satin stitch noses and eyes. Bring the needle out through point A, insert at point B, and repeat, following the shape you want for the nose or eyes and making sure to work the stitches really close together. Secure the ends on the wrong side.

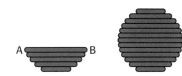

Another option for embroidering a nose is to work from a center point upward. Bring the needle up from underneath at point A; insert the needle at point B. Bring the needle up at point C, very close to point A. Insert the needle back into point B. Continue working stitches close to each other to create a triangle, making sure to always insert the needle back into point B. When you're satisfied with the triangle, make two long stitches across the top of the nose to help define it.

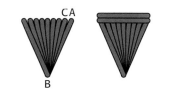

STUFFING

Stuff your toys firmly so they retain their shape and don't look "droopy." Be careful not to overstuff them, though, because the stuffing will stretch the fabric and may show through the stitches.

I always use polyester fiberfill stuffing because it's nonallergenic, won't bunch up, and it's washable, which is always good when you're making toys! If you do wash the toys, make sure you follow the yarn care instructions on the label.

For Tree Love on page 40, I used Poly-Pellets so the tree would stand on its own. See the sidebar on page 40.

ADDING THE EXTREMITIES

I always use a tapestry needle and the same color of yarn as the pieces (or at least one of the pieces) that I want to sew together. When sewing pieces to the body, make sure they are securely attached so that little fingers can't pull them off.

On some animals, the opening of the extremities will remain open for sewing onto the body; the instructions will tell you when to leave them open. Position the limb on the body and sew all around it, going through the front stitches of both the limb and the body.

On other animals, the opening of the extremities will be sewn closed before being attached to the body. To do this, pinch the opening closed, line up the stitches of one side with the other side, and sew through the front loop of one side and the back loop of the other side. Position the piece where you want it on the body and sew.

WEAVING IN ENDS

Weaving in ends is easy on little ami pieces. Because the pieces are stuffed, simply pull the tails to the inside of the piece and leave them. The tails will be secure inside the pieces. If there are any tails left after sewing the pieces together, insert the needle into the body, pull it out 1" or 2" away, and snip close to the piece, being careful not to cut the crochet stitches.

ABBREVIATIONS AND GLOSSARY

*	repeat directions between * and * as many times as indicated	**R**	round(s)/row(s)	**sl st**	slip stitch
BPsc	back-post single crochet	**rem**	remaining	**sp**	space
ch	chain	**rep**	repeat	**st(s)**	stitch(es)
dc	double crochet	**rnd**	round	**tog**	together
dec	decrease (see "Single Crochet Decrease" on page 74)	**RS**	right side	**tr**	triple crochet
hdc	half double crochet	**sc**	single crochet	**WS**	wrong side
		sk	skip		

RESOURCES

YARN

Caron

www.caron.com

Lion Brand Yarn

www.lionbrand.com

Patons

www.patonsyarns.com

Red Heart

www.coatsandclark.com

SAFETY EYES

Your local craft store probably carries safety eyes. If you can't find them locally, visit www.sunshinecrafts.com; search for "eyes." They ship them fast. If you want fun, colorful eyes, check out www.suncatchereyes.net.

ABOUT THE AUTHOR

Ana Paula Rímoli was born in Montevideo, Uruguay, where she was always making stuff. She started crocheting when she was little, sitting outside one summer afternoon with her neighbor lending instruction. She started with scarves and granny squares and little bags and never stopped.

When her oldest daughter was born, she started crocheting little toys for her and later discovered amigurumi. Ana's been "hooked" ever since, and the toy collection is growing and growing, slowly taking over the whole house!

Ana now lives in New Jersey with her two little girls and never-ending sources of inspiration, Oli and Martina; her little dog, Santiago; and her super-nice husband who supports her yarn obsession.

Ana is also the author of *Amigurumi World* (Martingale & Company, 2008) and *Amigurumi Two!* (Martingale & Company, 2009).

THERE'S MORE ONLINE!

Visit Ana's Etsy shop at www.anapaulaoli.etsy.com and her blog at www.amigurumipatterns.blogspot.com. Find more crochet and knitting books at www.martingale-pub.com.

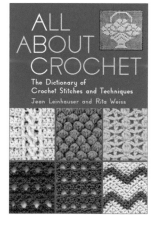
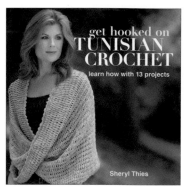